HOSTAGE of the MIND

KOREAN WAR MARINE'S SAGA OF WAR'S TRAUMA AND THE BATTLE THAT FOLLOWED HIM HOME....

P.T.S.D*.

***Post-Traumatic Stress Syndrome**

STAN MODRAK

Branden Books, Boston

Library of Congress Cataloguing-in-Publication Data

Modrak, Stan.
Hostage of the mind : Korean War marine's saga of war's trauma and the battle that followed him home : P.T.S.D., post-traumatic stress syndrome / Stan Modrak.
pages cm
Includes bibliographical references and index.
ISBN 978-0-8283-2460-1 (print edition) -- ISBN (invalid) 978-0-8283-2461-8 (e-book edition)
1. Modrak, Stan.
2. Korean War, 1950-1953--Personal narratives, American.
3. Marines--United States--Biography.
4. United States. Marine Corps--Biography.
5. Korean War, 1950-1953--Psychological aspects.
6. Korean War, 1950-1953--Veterans--Mental health--United States.
7. Post-traumatic stress disorder--Patients--United States--Biography.
8. Veterans--United States--Biography. I. Title.

DS921.6.M63 2012
951.904'245092--dc23
[B]

2012032212

ISBN 9780828324601 Paperback, ISBN 9780828324618 E-Book
Branden Books
P.O. Box 812094
Wellesley, MA 02482

www.brandenbooks.com

DEDICATION

To Jim, Judy and Bill

A much-appreciated triumvirate
of encouragement
time and technical assistance.

TABLE OF CONTENTS

PREFACE

As brooding grief assails and binds
Harboring disquiet reveries
The warrior's soul essays to find
Succor from dark memories.

Hostage of the Mind recounts the traumatic journey of the author, a Korean War Purple Heart Marine-a traumatic journey not only in war's milieu but a protracted journey through mental anguish--many years later. *Hostage of the Mind* is comprised of and relates both elements.

Part I relates how Marine Corps "Gung ho" spirit and *elan* led to volunteering for Korea – and war when the unexpected war broke on the world scene in June of 1950. It goes on to describe and recount the chaos, horror and traumatic events undergone by the author, a very young, very inexperienced combatant. The author's mind and body-shaking trauma occurred during the opening salvo of the vicious and casualty-ridden *Chosin Reservoir* campaign in North Korea. This historic first-ever meeting between Communist China's armed forces and the U.S. Marine Corps proved to be a crucial one.

Veterans Administration P.T.S.D. counselor, and friend, Mr. Bill Dolon, LMFT writes: "*There have been many literary efforts that speak of the reality of combat. Fueled by public awareness of present conflicts, an increasing number of these address the psychological baggage that the combat veteran returns with upon returning home. Hostage of the Mind relates the personal experience of the author, Stan Modrak in both arenas, lending "I've been there" credibility to each. The Korean conflict, an armed struggle devoid of parades and debate is referred to as the "Forgotten War." But it is this war's anonymous presence in public conscience that makes the author's narrative more poignant."*

Part II relates the debilitating effects of P.T.S.D. or *Post-Traumatic Stress Disorder.* P.T.S.D. is a mental illness borne of war's traumatic events demoralizing thousands of combat veterans of various wars all across the Nation.

No veterans of any era have been spared; WWII, Korea, Vietnam and now Gulf War military are affected. Known as "soldiers' heart" during the Civil war, "shell shock" in WWI, and "battle fatigue" in WWII, it's now referred to in psychiatric circles as P.T.S.D. Life disturbing depression, lachrymose grief, lack of concentration and an enervating lethargy of mind, body and spirit are common effects.

P.T.S.D. and its harpy-like handmaidens of grief and depression conjure up bleak clouds of wartime memories scudding through the mind. Now surging, now receding, a desultory tide crashing and breaking on the vulnerable shoals of sanity. A ravaging of mind and body, indeed a mental counter-point to *Prometheus'* unending physical torture not unlike his chaining to that eternal rock, the P.T.S.D. – laden veteran is mentally chained and held hostage by the mind's vagaries engendered by the intrusive, mind-altering malady called P.T.S.D.

The triggering and onset of P.T.S.D. is unpredictable at best. It may strike close to the wartime trauma – even 30-years later! One contributory factor is that many veterans bury their harrowing wartime traumas for years, deep in their psyche's darkens caverns where it lurks – waiting...waiting.

Dr. Jonathan Shay, mental health expert and counselor estimates that well over 33% of our thousands and thousands of our combat veterans have, or will develop this disturbing illness. Others feel that this malady affects a much larger percentage of veterans. They all agree however that P.T.S.D. is not completely curable, only managed and kept in control.

Chapter 1

Oh those "Dress Blues"

Have you ever had a "Memory Wall" in your home? I do and it evokes a variety of emotions, reveries and memories: The siren-song of adventure beckoning, the thrill of scaling troop-ship cargo nets into assault craft, the happy laughter of North Korean tots, the discordant and chilling blare of Red Chinese bugles, the stark effect of a traumatic wounding, meeting with a sports icon in the midst of a "Hot War", even happy, exhilarating times as a post-war civilian playing ice hockey.

One wall of my home's hallway features mementos that often conjure up the above-mentioned memories – both happy and sad. The provocative mementos are a Marine Corps "Dress Blues" jacket featuring the Purple Heart medal, an American League baseball autographed by Joe DiMaggio and an ice hockey jersey and puck with a painted numeral 'five' along with pertinent pictures.

In the bloom and verve of youth oftime we dream-chimera-like dreams of a lusty life begetting travel and adventure. Not long after High School graduation at St. Mary's of the Mount in Pittsburgh, Pa., the Marine Corps "Dress Blues"-adorned recruiting posters beckoned - "The Marines want you!" They soon had me – enlisting in June of 1948 less than three years from the end of horrific WWII. Another disturbing factor was living in McKeesport, a drab, soot-ridden steel community on the outskirts of Pittsburgh. A second stepmother and a rather aloof father held no future hopes either.

Actually, darn near didn't make it through my pre-induction physical exam. A recent football injury leaving me with a partially crooked left elbow resulting from a compound fracture was the culprit. In a room full of other enlistees the examining doctor had us strip to the waist and extend our arms forward; realizing that the crooked elbow would show and wash me out, I swiveled my arm so that the deformity was toward the side and wouldn't be as noticeable. Well, fortunately – or unfortunately considering what my four years in the Corps would have in store for me, I passed.

Soon we recruits were on our way to Marine Corps Recruit Depot or “Boot Camp” at Parris Island South Carolina. Not quite knowing what to expect, we arrived and were ushered into a room by a 'friendly' Marine sergeant shouting, “Awright you shitheads! Line up on those footprints on the floor -- move it!” Such was our introduction to Marine Corps boot camp discipline on a blistering hot day in South Carolina by our surly sergeant. Can't recall the dear fellow's name but he certainly made a huge impression. Especially 'consoling' was when assured with: “Your mother may have your heart, but the Marine Corps has your ass!” Welcome to the corps – what have I gotten myself into I mused.

After a ruthless Marine barber rendered us all completely bald we were issued clothing and bedding. Then we marched to our barracks 'home' by our D.I. Or Drill Instructor, a very sharp corporal named Rolle.

Ten weeks of boot camp ensued; close order drills, exercises, marches with full field packs and M-1 rifles amid South Carolina's sweat- inducing summer heat. During one march I passed out from the heat but was quickly revived, given salt tablets then 'comforted' with:”Ok boot, you've had your little siesta -NOW FALL IN!” Then there was that lovely interlude when the whole platoon was jam-packed and locked inside a small shack and given a taste of tear gas – without masks! Scary man, scary! When they finally opened the doors there was a mass exodus of bleary, tearing recruits fighting to get into fresh air.

Soon two weeks followed on the rifle range where <u>every Marine</u> was required to qualify with his M-1 rifle. The Marine Corp's overriding philosophy was that every Marine was <u>first a rifleman</u> no matter what his eventual rank and duty status. This basic philosophy proved its worth over time as in many tight combat situations cooks, bakers, HQ personnel and truck drivers would fill in as rifle-men to help “save the day.” In fact when Boston Red Sox Hall-of-Famer Ted Williams was asked by reporters during his stint in the Korean War what his duties entailed, he replied “I'm a marine rifle-man currently flying a F-86

Sabre jet."

Another interesting Korean War incident involving baseball's 'Splendid splinter' Ted Williams occurred as he was returning to base after a mission. Nearing the airfield, Yon-po as I recall, his Sabre jet began smoking profusely. Advising the control tower of his problem they directed him to "Bail out Williams.!" But Ted deferred saying, "I'm bringing it in – I'll break these long legs of mine if I try to eject from this cockpit." And bring it in did the intrepid Williams in a belly-sliding crash- landing -then walking away uninjured.

After boot camp graduation parade we returned to our barracks where we were issued the mark of accomplishment – our PFC or private first class chevrons along with our rifle range qualifying medals. After all the weeks of being demeaned, insulted we were now instilled with pride in ourselves and a feeling of self-worth. We felt that we were now that paragon of young manhood – a Marine: *Semper Fi*. Years later I realized that the Marine Corps training philosophy was innovative and well-perfected in turning young teens into healthy, proud and competent American warriors eager to serve our country and to achieve feats of derring-do and bravery when ever called upon.

During boot camp a battery of aptitude tests found me assigned to Marine Radio School at Camp Del Mar just north of San Diego in southern California. Though I enjoyed the idea of being a radio operator in beautiful and warm southern California, I had no idea of the ramifications and traumatic experiences that would occur later resulting from this new duty experience and training.

Preparing to leave on a 30-day post-boot camp leave, I was happy to learn that my best boot camp buddy, Johnny DeRennaux was also assigned to Radio School. Johnny was discouraged though that his long-time friend from their youth in St. Louis, Ray Lemmons was assigned somewhere else. Later, in this book, I'll relate the dire consequences of Ray's duty station elsewhere.

Radio School proved to be interesting and challenging for my comrades and I hoping to qualify as Marine radio operators. After some weeks of intensive classroom "Morse Code" practice we were gradually able to send, receive and type copy, even gain some speed.

On weekends we had some free time so my buddies and I experienced our first ocean swim enjoying the stimulating waters of the Pacific. Camp Del Mar sat close to the Pacific just a few yards beyond the coastal sand dunes. Another activity that we enjoyed on weekends was hitch hiking to either L. A. or San Diego not far from either city. We never had to wait long for a ride either as the local civilians were glad to accommodate the military.

Two of my buddies, Johnny DeRennaux, Fields and myself soon were befriended by a kind East L.A. Family, the Freemans, and spent some weekends in their home. They had a teen-age daughter, Mary Lou, that her mom was trying to help meet young men and we were available. Mary Lou however, was not that attractive and a little on the heavy side. But all in all we enjoyed their friendship, meals and weekends away from the rigors of our military duties. One thing in particular that I enjoyed was that I was able to experience my first taste of TV and on January 1st, 1949, enjoyed my first Rose Bowl game on TV.

After a few weeks of applying our new radio operators schooling we spent most of our time in field exercises among the coastal sand dunes along the Pacific.

Happy to complete our training, Johnny and I were given orders to report to Fleet Marine Force (FMF) at Camp Lejeune, North Carolina. Upon reporting we were assigned to *Anglico,* or Air, Naval Gunfire Liason Company. *Anglico* consisted of naval gunfire forward spotting teams and close air support spotting teams. My assignment was with a naval gunfire team.

Each *Anglico* spotting team, naval gunfire or close-air support usually consisted of the team officer usually a Lieutenant, a staff sergeant and three PFC radiomen. As a self-contained specialty company, the various spotting teams in combat roles would be dedicated to provide fire support, whether naval gunfire or air at the battalion level. These teams were assigned the important task of enhancing their battalion's firepower with timely and accurate targeting of naval shelling or fighter/bomber missions.

My particular naval spotting team utilized an ANGR-9 shore-to-ship radio powered by a hand-cranked generator. Each radioman would back-pack one of the radio components along with his field pack and weapon. Our team makeup consisted of Lt. Jones, one sharp Marine, an NCO and three radiomen. Willie Greene, Rex Farler and myself were radio school buddies fitting in well together.

All in all we found duty with Anglico stimulating and very interesting especially when we would go on fire-mission exercises at Onslow Beach and other Virginia venues. We would now actually call in live-fire missions to offshore cruisers. Not realized at the time these exercises and live-fire missions were a harbinger of things to come – and not too long in our future.

As my best pal Johnny was assigned to another spotting team we didn't get to see each other during most field exercises but did make up for it by usually going on liberty together or at base activities. Fortunately for us young guys, Camp Lejeune had a nice big movie theater showing current movies. We also got to enjoy a large swimming pool with 2-level diving boards on weekends. My diving wasn't the most graceful but it was a lot of fun trying.

Just for kicks when John Wayne's “Sands of Iwo Jima” played at our base theater we went to the movie all dressed up in our “Dress Blues.” Usually Marines only wear their 'Blues' for parades, out on liberty or for special occasions. I don't remember if others wore theirs.

Many of my readers may remember seeing newsreels of various Marine Corps assault landings on island beaches during WWII's Pacific campaign. They would climb down thick cargo nets on the sides of 'APA' troopships and into the 'LCVP' (landing craft vehicle/personnel) waiting below. This can be a little hairy at times especially when the once-tranquil Pacific Ocean decides to 'act up' with huge swells that can lift the landing craft waiting below in a violent up-and-down motion of sometimes six or eight feet at a time. I can personally attest to this having experienced this 'thrill' during some of our assault landing exercises in Hawaii and at Viequez Island in the Caribbean. One has to carefully time his release of the nets to drop into the LCVP's at the high point of the crafts upward surge. Otherwise, a badly timed drop could result in a possible eight-foot drop onto an unforgiving steel deck. With our field packs and radio gear on it could prove to be a helluva jolt, even injury. Fortunately I managed to survive a few of these 'Fun days at the beach' and later in Korea in good shape – even enjoyed them.

I must say that the two-mentioned assault landing exercises at Oahu in Hawaii and Viequez Island in the Caribbean also did provide some fun. One fun incident that I didn't participate in, only heard of it later was when 'Bud' Smith, a blond, good-natured kid from Omaha, Nebraska, somehow managed to catch and ride one of Viequez' wild ponies that roamed the island. Don't remember though the results of his 'wild ride.' Later in the book I'll relate another event involving Smith, his buddy Billy Johnson, both in Captain Stamford's close-air spotting team -this time resulting in dire consequences.

Another fun time was after the conclusion of the Hawaii exercises when we all had liberty to enjoy a swim at Waikiki Beach – very pleasant memory indeed. When Operation Viequez ended we again boarded ship sailing to Kingston, Jamaica for a day and evening of shore liberty. Kingston was very British with native traffic people, tall and impressive with elaborate uniforms and be-medaled pith helmets. I can still recall that warm afternoon enjoying exotic drinks with some of my buddies on the back patio of a splendid hotel. Right on the beach we could enjoy the beautiful, blue Caribbean waters as their sands formed a curvature around our hotel. That evening we further enjoyed a bit of Jamaican night-life at a restaurant and bar that featured local music.

Well all good things have to come to an end, don't they? We were soon aboard ship headed back to Camp Lejeune. On the way back our ship traversed the Panama Canal. What a thrilling experience you might think. Well it was, but not for me! Myself and another Marine were relegated to scullery duty in the ship's mess area below decks and never got to see the Canal. Whether this was due to some mean Navy officer or an unthinking Marine officer, I never did find out.

Chapter 2

War!

Summer of 1950 found us enjoying a lull in Anglico operations. We now had time to follow baseball box scores in the daily papers following our favorite teams from afar. The closest Major League team was the Former Washington Senators. We also had time on the ball field, or for some swimming at the base indoor pool: a beautiful pool, very wide and long with two diving boards.

June 25th we were relaxing in our Camp Lejeune barracks "shooting the breeze", shining our shoes or listening to the Washington Senator's ballgame on the radio or reading the papers. Then it happened! Bulletin! A sudden deadly war has broken out as ten North Korean army divisions supported with the famous Russian T-34 tanks have invaded the Republic of South Korea. At this time the South Korean Army was ill-equipped and badly trained. Well-trained, well-equipped North Korean Army swept over the border and through the Oijongbu corridor with little resistance. The South Korean Capitol of Seoul fell within a few days. Word that the United Nations has called an emergency meeting soon followed. Naturally we were all shocked and surprised by the unexpected military action. That day and the next our barracks was alive with excited conjectures and "scuttlebutt" rumors. We wondered how this dire turn of events would affect the United States and our Marine Corps.

.Within days, "The Word" came down. Camp Lejeune was quickly galvanized into action and preparations as President Harry S. Truman (we Marines called him 'hairy ass') ordered the Corps to immediately form an emergency contingent for orders. The 1st Marine Brigade was formed under General Craig and prepared to head to Korea. South Korea at the time was in our post-war treaty organization known as SEATO or Southeast Asia Treaty Organization.

We Marines had no love for President Truman as he had been

wrong-headedly calling for the elimination of the Marine Corps. It had to be inter-military jealousy due to the Marine Corps heroic and well-chronicled exploits throughout the Pacific campaigns at Guadalcanal, Iwo Jima, Tarawa, etc.

The call came down from Division for volunteer Anglico close-air and naval gunfire spotting teams to also prepare for Korea in support of Marine forward ground units. We have a long-standing saying in the Corps: “Don't volunteer for anything!” Traditional admonitions and common sense not-withstanding, my team buddies and I all did volunteer for Korea along with other Anglico spotting teams. Looking back, most volunteers were well aware of the Korean Peninsula's location near China and Japan. But we had no idea of the rugged hills, and mountainous landscape that we'd soon be facing and struggling to overcome.

At this time our team consisted of a Lieutenant Jones, a staff sergeant, Cpl's Willie Greene, Rex Farler and myself. We'd been together since radio school and got on well with each other. Hailing from Keokuk, Iowa, Rex was on the quiet side but good - natured. Willie, from somewhere in Michigan was very gregarious, one of those always smiling, happy kids. I guess that I could admit to being a little on the introverted side.

Though anxious for some adventure in exotic environments and 'Gung-ho' to go, I was disappointed to learn that Johnny DeRennaux, my best buddy, was exempted from going overseas as he had recently married and his enlistment had less than a year to go. The rest of us three-year enlistees were 'frozen' for an extra year by Congress. We also learned that Lt. Jones and our team NCO were not going to Korea. Why, I never found out. The change came from 'upstairs', who knows.

“Gung-ho” and fired up for our first taste of high adventure, we packed our gear, wrote letters home and were soon on our way, entrained for sunny Southern California and Camp Pendleton. Upon arriving, after a few days, we were assigned to the 7th Marine Regiment now being quickly fleshed out with almost 50% Marine Reserves hurriedly called up. A unique tribute to the Marine Corps is that its leadership, discipline, training and *Esprit de Corps* enables regulars and reservists to meld into a capable, confident fighting force almost immediately. Many of the regular and reserve officers and NCO's were WWII veterans with valuable combat leadership experience during the Pacific campaigns. This cadre of experienced leadership was headed up by Lewis "Chesty" Puller, our greatest fighting Marine.

Our team didn't have much time to get to know our newly-assigned team leaders, a Lieutenant and Staff Sergeant but it didn't bother us. Traditionally most Marines have complete confidence in their officers and Non-Coms almost taking for granted their abilities, experience and leadership. I'm sorry to say that one of the still-troubling memories of Korea is that I cannot remember our team leaders' names. I've felt over the ensuing years almost a shame for not honoring their names. Later, in the P.T.S.D. chapters I relate the dolorous incident involving them to cause me to bury their names.

Arriving at the San Diego docks with our field packs, radio gear and weapons we boarded an APA (Assault Personnel troop ship). As we prepared to leave, the Marine Band serenaded us with *Goodnight Irene,* a popular song at the time. After the fanfare subsided, it was "Up Anchor" and a ship full of excited young Marines and their officers were on their way to their "Oriental Odyssey."

After settling in in our quarters and having chow, we had time to relax in our of the upper deck's social areas. I still recall vividly during one evening of socializing and music how a strapping, 6-foot plus Marine led us in a rousing chorus of *New York, New York.* I sometimes muse; did he make it home to his beloved New York. Looking back I regret not keeping some sort of diary to savor after the war. Names, places, events along with recalling feelings and emotions during Korea would be especially gratifying.

The crossing was uneventful; lifeboat drill, letter writing, card games and the reserves preparing for war practicing firing their M-1 rifles from the ship's fantail.

Mid-September we arrived in Japan docking in Kobe Harbor. We were given one evening of liberty ashore to 'enjoy' the wonders of the Orient before heading to Korea the next morning. Kobe was typical of post-war Japan, crowded streets bustling with humanity. Interspersed among the drab, dimly lit streets, painted ladies dressed in colorful kimonos strolled here and there, laughing and giggling as we Marines waved and beckoned. I'm not saying if we had any 'luck.'

Stopping at a local bar we savored our first taste of Saki as three young Japanese men approached us. Speaking English well, one of them told us that they knew we were headed for Korea and wished that they could also go and help America--a surprising example of American/Japanese amity only five years after defeating Tojo and the Japanese Empire. I wonder though, was this gesture on their part a sign of friendship for America or hatred for the Korean people.

Safely back aboard ship, the next day just before sailing we heard 'scuttelbutt' (Rumors) that a Marine was found dead floating in Kobe Harbor. Never did hear of any confirmation though. The "Big Adventure" that we volunteered for began very early as our APA sailed for South Korea.

Excitement and spirit seemed evident to me as I scanned the faces of my buddies and other Marines as we neared our destination. As for myself I felt a nervous excitement welling up within but no fears or any sense of foreboding – didn't know any better not having experience war or its traumatic effects. The "word" came down that we were headed for an assault landing at Inchon, an industrial port city about 15 to 20 miles west of Seoul, South Korea's Capitol.

The Inchon landing was General Douglas MacArthur's brilliant "End Run" strategy, a military gambit that effectively cut off the threatening North Korean Army at the 'Pusan perimeter' at the southern end of the Korean Peninsula. Learning of the Inchon landing would send North Korea's Pusan force fleeing north, abandoning their hopes of conquering all of South Korea and winning the war. They fled north to escape being trapped and destroyed between the U.S. Army southern forces and the 1st Marine Division's assault landing at Inchon.

An interesting prelude to the actual Inchon strategic assault occurred. At a meeting at Wake Island with President Truman, Chief-of Staff generals and high-echelon admirals, General MacArthur, who had been dubbed "The American Caesar" by author William Manchester, using his superb confident leadership borne of his WWII successes and reputation, won out over

Truman's and others doubts.

Preceded by the Division's 1st and 5th Regiments by a few days, our 7th Regiment came ashore about mid-September at Wolmi-do Island. A small, cone-shaped island, Wolmi-do was separated from Inchon proper by a narrow stone causeway. The 5th Marines had secured the island except for some mopping-up with a little clearing out some enemy snipers.

In addition Marine fighters and fighter-bombers had complete control of the air. They left Kimpo airfield, the only major airfield in the area a complete shambles; devastated hangers and burning aircraft littering the runways.

After our team crossed the narrow stone causeway into Inchon proper, now in the process of being secured by "Chesty" Puller's 5th Marines along with our 7th Regiment, we began moving inland along the main road leading east to Seoul, South Korea's Capitol city. Shortly we passed five smoldering hulks of T-34 tanks killed by the preceding regiment. I later learned that two of the enemy tanks had been killed by a valiant bazooka-man, PFC Walter Monaghan before giving up his own life. Monaghan had repeatedly exposed himself in his daring efforts to get close enough for a kill – and kill he did, leaving two T-34 tanks afire and destroyed. He was later awarded the Medal of Honor, posthumously.

Our first night at war found us climbing a steep hill, typical of the Korean landscape, to dig in for the night. Lugging full field packs, radio gear and weapons it proved to be quite an exhausting ascent. As we began digging in – what a macabre experience! We began to unearth human remains and bones. Unknowingly, in the pitch-black darkness we had stumbled into a cemetery! After our efforts to dig in, the rest of our first memorable night in Korea passed without incident.

Next day's evening we were trucked into the Kimpo Peninsula, northwest of Inchon and the site of the main Inchon/Seoul airfield. Destroyed hangers and some wrecked and burning enemy aircraft that littered the area were a testament to our destructive air and naval bombardments. The Division had assigned our team to help support the Army's 187th Airborne unit with naval gunfire missions from our offshore cruisers and battleships. Soon our team had the memorable experience of live fire missions.

The Army's 187th Airborne unit that we were attached to had the mission of clearing the Kimpo Peninsula of enemy guerilla forces made up of North Korean regulars that had been flushed from the Inchon battle area and now relegated to night harassing attacks. These enemy forces had doffed their uniforms for the usual white civilian attire, hide by day and then attempt night time ambushes of our forces. In fact, one of our wire-laying teams also attached to the 187th was ambushed one night, taking casualties but thankfully no KIA's. One of our wounded as I recall was a PFC Watkins I knew from radio/wire-laying school. The fall of darkness now became more ominous and we all made sure that our .45 automatics and M-1 carbines were loaded and readily at hand.

Soon we had the exciting experience of not only calling in fire missions, but with the U.S.S Missouri WWII's famous 'Mighty Mo' battleship shortly after joining up with a 187th unit on the crest of a tall hill. The hill overlooked a wide valley containing a large village about ten miles in the distance. The 187th had learned that this particular village had become a haven for enemy guerillas, setting up ambushes by night and returning by daylight to the village, now disguised as white-clad villagers. This particular Army unit we joined had suffered casualties from these guerilla incursions including KIA's. As young, inexperienced kids, seeing our first bodies of the 187th's KIA's was quite a sobering sight as you may imagine. My buddies and I now realized that war was deadly serious and that death could call at any moment in any situation.

Setting up our radio and generator, our team officer made contact with a waiting battleship offshore. As I mentioned earlier, the U.S.S. Missouri was standing by for immediate fire missions. After studying area coordinates and making calculations our army officer radioed the Missouri to prepare for a fire mission.

When calling in naval gunfire the procedure was to use just a single shell to establish a fire base. Our officer would then call for another shell after directing adjustments in increments of 50 yards: 50 yards up, down, left or right. When satisfied that the shells were on target or close, he would radio "Fire for effect!" The Missouri would then let go a salvo or four or six 16" shells. The ensuing explosions were devastating, raising huge clouds of red and black in or near the village. In my mind's eye even to this day I can see those explosions and dozens of tiny, white-clad figures fleeing from the village. Each 16” shell can create a crater as large as a tennis court. Each huge shell passing overhead sounded like the loud rumbling of a freight train.

Another day we were directed to hit another target nearby. By some miscalculations, or by some faulty information, this fire mission was almost a disaster. Our first directed shell landed and exploded very near an Army unit. No casualties but angry messages from somewhere higher up. We were then pulled out of the Kimpo area and returned to our regimental control. We never learned the why of the screw-up but it did get us back with our 7th Regiment. All in all, our baptism of calling in 16” shell fire missions from the 'Mighty Mo” turned out to be an exciting and eventful experience.

Glad to return to our 7th Regiments control, we rejoined Col. Homer Litzenberg's regiment at Yongdongpo, an industrial city somewhere between Inchon and Seoul. As our regiment was now in the process of re-supplying and re-fitting we had a few days to relax and enjoy some hot chow. For a change, we learned the welcome news that Seoul had been liberated in less than a month, another well-deserved honor in General MacArthur's successful career. While at Yongdongpo we learned that Truman's reluctance re: the Inchon Landing was that Inchon's harbor and landing areas could prove to be dangerous for our landing craft due to prevailing low tides.

Chapter 3

Fow Bah!

Shortly after arriving at Yongdopo a happy incident occurred. A little South Korean tyke, maybe six or seven years old showed up in our bivouac area in a bombed-out mill. Apparently he had heard that American military were kind to kids, giving them food and sometime gum or candy bars. We took to the little guy immediately and now that we had hot chow we would let our new-found friend come into the chow line with us. We realized as did our officers that the bedraggled and hungry Korean children were all war-deprived victims and felt sorry for them. Unlike the cruel North Korean People's Army (NKPA) who would steal food supplies from the South Korean civilian population.

Our team, all young teenagers, took to the little tyke and dubbed him "Peanuts." Being only dressed in rags, we 'liberated' some Marine dungarees jacket and cap. The smallest jacket we could come up with hung on his little frame almost down to his knees, but he didn't seem to mind, smiling broadly all the while. Even though Peanuts couldn't speak English and we had only picked up very few words of the Korean language, with a little practice with sign language we were able to communicate well enough to be understood. Peanuts would light with a big grin when Willie or Rex would call out to him "Chow Peanuts!" Our new little mascot wasted no time in heading to the chow line.

After about a week or so in bivouac, out team sergeant called us together and came up with some news. "Ok, you guys; get your gear squared away and get ready – we're shipping out for North Korea!"

"Wow! Let's go" we cheered as by now we were getting bored with inaction, never considering the possibility of what danger might be in store for us .Then as young, unsophisticated kids we showed our lack of military experience by trying to take little Peanuts with us up north. Thinking that we could get away with such a ridiculous idea we took him to his parent's home in Seoul to ask for their permission to take their little boy with us up north. Short of food, they agreed readily.

Of course it was ridiculous to try and we had to sadly part with our downcast little friend and mascot. I thought of little Peanuts often, hoping that he survived the Communist Reds recapture of Seoul that re-occurred in 1951. I especially worried if the Reds were to see him in Marine dungarees.

Boarding a Japanese LST, a gift to Japan after WWII, now used in Korean War troop movements, we were soon on our way north glad to be heading for new adventures. The full and horrific impact of war on us was yet to come. Headed for the North Korean port of Wonsan high up on the east coast of North Korea we finally found ourselves delayed for days. Our minesweepers had to clear mines from Wonsan's harbor before we could land safely. As our LST sailed back and forth for days we called this delay "Operation Yo-Yo." This back and forth movement sure led to a lot of sick Marines I'll tell you. If I remember correctly I think that I did ok though.

Upon finally landing at Wonsan Harbor, unopposed, we learned that American screen star Bob Hope and his Hollywood entertainment troupe had beat the Marines to Wonsan! Leave it to good old Bob Hope along with comedienne Jerry Colona and some Hollywood 'lookers' to upstage the Marine Corps! Humorous though embarrassing and disappointing to our regiment, to this day missing seeing Bob Hope in a war zone remains one of my many Korean War regrets. That darn Operation Yo-Yo.

Not long after entering Wonsan Harbor and debarking, Rex came up with some very unexpected 'scuttlebutt' or rumor during chow. "Hey guys, I just heard from a Headquarters guy in chow line that the war is winding down and we'll all be home for Christmas!" Little did we know at the time that the rumor would turn out to be just wishful thinking: not only that, but not expected by any of us was that our most harrowing Korean War experience was yet to come.

Shortly the 7th Marines and our team started moving up the coastal road to the port city of Hungnam. Now late October we were all saddened to hear shocking news of the death of one of our

Anglico comrades, Cpl. Fish. We learned that an element of "Chesty" Puller's 1st Marines, some miles south on the coast, were hit by a surprise night overrun by the NKPA guerilla forces. The marine unit was quickly overrun with many bayoneted in their sleeping bags! Sadly, Cpl. Fish was one of our Marines bayoneted to death while struggling to unzip and clear his sleeping bag. Fish was one of Anglico's quiet, decent guys and his horrible death hit us all hard – still does.

However, we also had an uplifting experience during our respite between campaigns -- one of those 'Feel Good' stories that rarely occur in war's combat zone. One warm and sunny afternoon our team had some time on our hands while 'enjoying' some C-Rations. While we were relaxing and 'shooting the breeze' as Marines put it, Rex came over. "Hey guys, let's see what's going on over there," he said, pointing to a small dirt field nearby. It seemed that 15 or 16 little North Korean tykes, maybe seven or eight years old, were laughing and chattering happily while running around in the dirt field Bedraggled and completely barefoot, the kids were playing soccer trying to use a small, round stone for a ball and didn't seem to mind at all.

"Isn't this something?" I remarked to my smiling buddies. "Here we are, right in the middle of a war zone and these little guys playing soccer without a care in the world." "And, what a difference after Inchon."

Rex agreed, "Just a couple of weeks ago we were calling in 16" shellfire, and now would you believe, a bunch of happy little kids laughing and playing a soccer game."

With the cheerful scene temporarily distracting our thoughts from war, I had an idea. "What do you say we try to teach these little guys some good old American baseball?" Pointing to some trees nearby, I told Willie:"Why don't you break off a branch from that nearby tree about the right size and shape for a kid-size bat while I ball up and tape up some socks for a ball." Rex decided to join in and began gathering up four thin stones, and voila! - We had home plate and bases.

Communicating wasn't a barrier either as with some sign language and motioning the kids caught on quickly. "Rex, take half the kids and show them field positions while Willie and I take the other half as batters." The kids seemed to be about the same size and age so it worked out fine.

Now ready to "Play Ball!" I suggested that Willie toss me a few pitches as I demonstrated how to hold a bat, step up to the plate and swing at a pitch. By now, all the kids' eyes were wide with wonder, watching these strange going-on. We were soon ready for our "historic" first Korean leadoff batter, Willie picked an eager, tiny guy we nicknamed Mickey.

Watching intently how I held the bat and faced the pitcher, Willie, he quickly followed suit, smiling happily all the while. All his buddies were giggling by this time watching what might happen. Spreading his little legs, Mickey struck a determined pose just as an American Little Leaguer might do. "Hey look at that, he sure learns fast" laughed Rex. Yeah, I agreed, looks like a miniature "Casey at the bat" all right. You parents reading this who've had the humorous experience of seeing your own Little Leaguer during their memorable initial at bat in a game can relate to this scene I'm sure.

Swinging wildly, little Mickey missed the first two pitches accompanied by "Oohs and aahs" from his playmates. After adjusting his swing I pointed to his eyes and then to the ball saying, "Keep your eyes on the ball Mickey."

Now getting the idea, Mickey hit the next two pitches except they rolled foul to the right. After each foul ball he hit I shouted "Foul Ball" to give them the idea. As it turned out, teaching them "Foul Ball" backfired in a humorous way. From then on every ball Mickey managed to hit, fair or foul, all the kids would shout "**Fow Bah!"** and laugh uproariously. The rest of our little game that fun afternoon in North Korea, every ball any of the kids would manage to hit, fair or foul, long or short, they missed no opportunity to shout "**Fow Bah!"** laughing and giggling happily.

Though only one brief afternoon interlude in North Korea, Rex, Willie and I got a huge kick out of their innocent joy and humorous take on American baseball. Imagine, right in a war zone area sharing baseball with little North Korean children – what a memory! You'll never hear many "Feel good" stories in the midst of war that's for sure – but we had one.

Today, though many years later, in the midst of somber wartime musing, vivid memories of little Mickey and his 15 or 16 little friends gleefully shouting **"Fow Bah!"** giggling happily still gladdens my heart, can yet bring on a big smile.

Addendum

Less than 30 years later, the first native Korean baseball player, pitcher Chan Ho Park, made it to the Major Leagues with the National League Los Angeles Dodgers. By now, a few other native Koreans have also made the grade to the Major Leagues. In fact, at the 2008 Summer Olympics the South Korean National team *won the Gold Medal!* Do you suppose that a trio of young American Marines, long, long ago, could have planted the seed?

Chapter 4
Many, many Chinese

I'd rather have a good Marine – even a ruined one – on my side when the chips are down.
Ernest Hemingway

As each November nears and northern California's blue skies and wind-blown clouds flee, surrendering to a glowering, gray overcast; I recall a bleak fall of 1950 in North Korea. Disquiet memories intrude; discordant bugles blaring, echoing from hill-to-hill high above; sudden shock and fear as fingers of death clutch; a shadowy figure hovering.

November 1st 1950

As young Marine Corps radiomen comprising an *Anglico* naval gunfire forward spotting team, November found us attached to the 2nd Battalion of Col. Homer Litzenberg's 7th Marine Regiment of Gen. O.P. Smith's 1st Marine Division. Our regiment was the lead regiment in the division's drive to reach the lofty and desolate Taebaek Plateau, leading to the *Chosin Reservoir.* The ultimate goal for our regiment and the division was to traverse the desolate Taebaek Mountains, secure the Chosin Reservoir, then continue northwest over the mountainous spine of North Korea to eventually link up with the U.S. 8th Army driving up the western side of the Korean Peninsula. Col. Lewis "Chesty" Puller's 1st Marine Regiment along with Lt. Col. Ray Murray's 5th Marines would follow.

After a day-long trek climbing a narrow, single-lane dirt road rising northwest, Col. Litzenberg chose a small, rock-strewn valley just south of a North Korean hamlet called Sudong-ni (town by the river) to bivouac his regiment for the night. The tiny valley was bordered on the road's left by a dry, rocky riverbed of the Changjin River traced by narrow-gauge rails. Sharply-rising hills dominated both sides of the road, designated the MSR or main supply road.

Peleliu veteran and Navy Cross winner, Lt. Col. Ray Davis positioned his 1st Battalion among a low hill mass to the front they called "boomerang hill". Davis set up his CP to the rear in a small ravine that afforded a good defilade. Major Webb Sawyer's 2nd Battalion in the valley's center, had his rifle companies dig in on the slopes of Hill 698 to the road's left and Hill 727 to the right. About a hundred yards or so to the rear, Litzenberg set up his regimental CP along with Major Maurice Roach's 3rd Battalion behind a low hill mass where the MSR curved to the left. Regimental artillery also set up there.

Our spotting team, attached to Major Sawyer's 2nd Bn. parked our jeep near the valley's center at the edge of the riverbed and set up our positions for the night. For some reason our team officer and sergeant had gone up into the nearby hills to spend the night with Leatherneck rifle companies. Unfortunately this decision was to prove disastrous for both.

It was a cardinal rule in the Marine Corps that each night in the field was considered a night of potential combat; establishing a viable communication net, and placing each machine gun to form an endless crossfire over every reachable square foot fronting their lines.

During chow line with evening approaching fast, we heard scuttlebutt rumors that Red Chinese troops had been contacted nearby by Republic of Korea (ROK) units. Actually the ROK's 26th Regiment that we were replacing had indeed run into Chinese soldiers, taking 16 prisoners. The Red Chinese were clad in quilted uniforms, mustard color on one side and winter white on the reverse side. They wore fur-lined caps with ear flaps and most had *canvas* shoes with crepe soles that our Marines called tennis shoes--couldn't understand the shoes in North Korean winter. Upon this disturbing news, Litzenberg met with his officers. With Chinese forces - "many, many Chinese "– as the ROKS put it, unexpectedly this far south and with contact possible, he cautioned his officers: "It's extremely important for Marines to win any first meeting with Red Chinese armed forces!"

As an added comment, Litzenberg told his officers; "Whoever

comes out ahead in such a crucial clash, the repercussions will reverberate around the world and in Peiping and Moscow as well." Being just a naval gunfire spotting team attached at Battalion level, of course we weren't in on any of this regimental info or philosophies.

Another piece of scuttlebutt circulating was that Col. Litzenberg, a gruff veteran officer, had once said: "The only Marines I want in my outfit are Purple Heart Marines!" Not fully realized by his young Marines, his words were soon to prove almost prophetic.

As the deep mountain darkness began to cloak the valley and surrounding hills, the rapidly cooling air signaled the approach of brutal North Korean weather soon to be howling down from sinister Manchuria. Unknown to the young Leathernecks, they were soon to be facing tortuous -20 % to -30% weather lashing the Taebaek Plateau and Chosin Reservoir area. Why the hell Gen. Almond, head of X-Corps, of which the 1st Marine Division was a component of, would order a Marine Division completely out of their element, into desolate mountains along a single-lane, twisting dirt road was incomprehensible to Marine leaders. The results of this wrong-headed decision would lead to future clashes between our Gen. Smith and the Army's Gen. Almond.

As the crisp, darkening night air found the 7th Marines breaking out sleeping bags and preparing for sleep, strains of *Goodnight Irene* filtered through our bivouac area as Rex pulled in Armed Forces Radio Tokyo in our radio jeep. The poignant melody evoked nostalgia for our homes as we recalled the Marine Band's goodbye serenade as we embarked from San Diego for Korea.

Meanwhile, unknown to the slumbering Marines, the Red Chinese 124th Infantry Division of General Sung's 42nd Field Army poised its 186th and 187th Regiments to hit Marine hill positions in a classic military *Double Envelopment.*

Burp-gun armed infantry and grenadiers poured toward the dug-in Marines on Hill698 left of the road, "Boomerang Hill" in the front of the valley, and Hill727 to the right, urged on by the Red's Gen. Sung's exhortation: "Kill these Marines as you kill snakes in your homes." Well, Gen.Sung and his minions would soon learn that "these Marines" had quite a nasty bite!

11:30 p.m.

"Here they come!"

Jolted awake by the unexpected shouts, we scrambled from our sleeping bags arming ourselves with MI Carbines and .45's. As radiomen having to lug radio equipment along with our field gear, we weren't armed with the heavier MI rifles.

A blare of discordant bugles echoed eerily from hill-to-hill above. Soon shadowy forms rose from the murky darkness in the riverbed to our left. As we let go with a fusillade of weaponry the forms faded into the deepening gloom. Rex, to my right, stood up and emptied his carbine on full automatic. Brave but foolish not knowing how many of the enemy might be near us. I marveled at the guts of our battalion officers as they stood tall in the valley's center directing their Marines defenses even though parachute flares exploding overhead bathed the tiny valley in a ghostly yellowish aura.

As mountain rivulets unleashed by a spring thaw form, multiply and then rush downhill following paths of least resistance, so too came the Red Chinese. Breaking past and veering around strong points relentless bands of quilt-garbed Chinese infantry cascades into, through and around Leatherneck hill positions intent on swarming into the valley floor battalion CP's.

1st. Lt. John Yancey, who would later earn the Navy Cross at Chosin, along with pvts. John Gallagher and Stanley Robinson, bravely withstood dozens of Reds, driving them from the crest of Hill 698 with a fusillade of accurate rifle and B.A.R. Fire; then broke up the ensuing counterattack. Col. Davis' voice rang out; "We expect an enemy attack any minute now. Check your ammo, dig in and remember, we're all Marines and we'll fight like Marines – good shooting!"

Not long afterwards after relative quiet, in the deep darkness a loud clanking mechanical noise broke the silence. It drowned out the enemy bugles across the riverbed. "Tank!" shouted S/Sgt. Don Jones. "These ears have heard a lot of Jap tanks in my day and that's a tank and its right in front of us." The armed intruder barreled right down the road straight at the surprised Marines with no accompanying infantry. Battalion AT weapons blazed away at her as she destroyed a roadblock with a direct blast from her 85mm rifle. Sandbags covering her hull and turret caught fire as she suddenly turned around trailing fiery sparks and clanked back up the road as quickly as she had appeared. Soon quiet settled in as the nervous Marines returned to their positions.

At the head of the embattled valley, Baker Co's platoon S/Sgt. Archie Van Winkle, though badly wounded, charged through 40 yards of the fire-swept hillside leading his squad to rescue cut-off Marines. Grenade shrapnel tore a hole in his left shoulder blade; then a bullet hit his back. Van Winkle still fought on, alternately firing his MI rifle and pistol using his good arm. A grenade exploded on his chest, breaking every rib on his left side. Breathing laboriously, he still encouraged his men until finally collapsing. The heroic Van Winkle survived his harrowing experience and was later awarded our nation's highest honor, the *Medal of Honor.*

Reaching the valley's floor, Chinese infantry overran Mortar Company positioned between First and Second Battalions. Mortarmen, some in hand-to-hand clashes, did heroic work slowing the enemy, enabling Second Battalion riflemen and machine gunners to set up a defensive line. Parachute flares exploded overhead, lighting the valley in a ghostly aura outlining clusters of Chinese infantry. B.A.R.'s and machine gunners let go a withering fire. Volumes of rifle fire interspersed with the staccato rattle of machine guns rose to an almost maddening, hellish din.

The once-quiet vale was now transformed into a vortex of hellish fury. Red (Marine) and green (Chinese) tracers laced the smothering darkness in a spectacular – and deadly – light show. Still with my team buddies at the edge of the riverbed, as the flares descended into the valley' center, we positioned ourselves to cover the riverbed expecting enemy infiltrating infantry to appear at any moment.

"One of you, come with me!" shouted a noncom rushing over to our position. Tossing a quick "Let's go- over there!" he motioned across the valley floor to our right. Marine discipline kicked in as I took off in a low, crouching run. Though only 50 or 60 yards or so across, it seemed like a hundred as skittering tracers crossed the pitch-black night. An almost maddening crash of gunfire seemed to fill every inch of mind and space. Never before or since, have I ever experience such an all-consuming, mind battering sound. I felt certain that a Chinese slug would tear into me any second before I could reach my destination across the valley. Years later, when dark memories of the Sudong Valley intrude, I still recall vividly the hellish din surrounding me undergoing that scary "Gauntlet" of fire.

Miraculously making it across untouched, I dove into the shadows behind a low stone wall at the base of a darkened hill mass. Expecting to be overrun at any moment, I checked my .45 for a full clip of ammo, laying an extra clip on the wall's ledge, ready for some fast and furious shooting.

When the burst struck, slamming into my side and forearm, I never saw my assailant, never clearly heard the shots! Sound, feeling, disbelief all jumbled together in a disjointed sensation as I realized that I was hit – and badly! As a bloody flow gathered under my parka, a sickening, enervating weakness took hold. "Corpsman!" I tried to shout, but tiring rapidly only a murmur emerged. Marines nearby took up the call as I slumped to the rocky earth. With consciousness rapidly fading, Col. Litzenberg's words; "Only Marines ... my outfit ... Purple Heart" were my last thoughts.

Reviving sometime later in the still smothering darkness, I sensed a shadowy form hovering over me. Was it an enemy, a fellow Marine, or ...? Quiet, firmly enunciated words broke the chill night air; "*In nomine, Patris, et Filii, et Spiritus Sancti, amen.*" I then realized that the form must be our Regimental Chaplain, Father "Connie" Griffin pronouncing the *Last Rites* of the Catholic Church. Growing up through twelve years of Catholic schooling I knew full well their dire implications. "Am I dying, Father"? I murmured. Passing out once again, I never heard any response.

Awakening the next morning to daylight in a med tent with other litter-bound wounded, it sure felt reassuring to be still among the living—also, no significant pain in my side that took two of the three rounds. Relief was short-lived however. Crack! Crack! Dirt began kicking up in the tent's dirt floor only a few feet from my litter! What a helpless feeling not knowing where the next shot would hit. "Sniper!" yelled a corpsman. They began putting helmets on the litter-bound wounded to hopefully provide some sort of protection as the intermittent firing continued. Being half-out-of-it, I don't know if Chaplain Griffin was in our med tent while the sniping was going on. Foolishly, our Navy surgeon opened the tent's flap to look outside. Crack! "Ugh!" he bent over in pain as a slug tore into his thigh! Soon the desultory fire ceased as we learned that Fox Company was busy clearing the snipers from a nearby hill. "Whew, thank God," I said to myself.

That night or the next, I don't know for sure as I was mostly unconscious, I awoke to find myself and three other litter-bound Marine wounded being loaded into a jeep rigged for four litters. Apparently our regiment had reopened the MSR allowing for evacuation of our casualties back down the road to 1st Marine Division Hospital at Hungnam on the coast.

Sometime later, still cloaked in deep darkness, our jeep skidded to a jarring stop. Jolted awake, we saw a Chinese soldier sitting on our jeep's hood attempting to light a cigarette! Our Marine driver, waving his .45 automatic menacingly, shouted "Light that damn cigarette and I'll blow your goddam head off!" He realized that Chicom stragglers still roamed the hills above and that a lit cigarette could be seen even from high above. I suppose that the Chicom soldier had been taken prisoner sometime during the Sudong battle and was being sent to Division Intelligence for questioning. Thankfully we made it back safely to Hamhung thanks to our intrepid driver's heady understanding action.

November Four signaled the end of the historic and bloody Sudong-ni valley action. Decimated remnants of the two CCF regiments withdrew north some three miles or so. A thunderous Marine Artillery barrage poured 1430 rounds in 49 fire missions. With over 1500 killed or wounded, Gen. Sung's 124th Infantry Division was rendered ineffective and withdrawn from action for the war's balance.

With another heroic victorious chapter added to the Marine Corps illustrious history, Col. Litzenberg's 7th Marine Regiment began to re-supply and prepare to resume their drive to the Chosin Reservoir. The regiment's casualties were over 60 KIA and some 300 WIA. Later, many historians felt that the victorious Sudong-ni outcome melded the 7th Marine regulars and, reservists into a veteran, confident fighting force at the Chosin Reservoir battle as the Inchon/Seoul Campaign did for Gen. O.P. Smith's 1st and 5th Regiments under the Veteran Col. “Chesty” Puller and Lt. Col. Ray Murray.

Addendum

An interesting and unusual incident took place during the Sudong-ni first daylight action. A large group of Chinese soldiers were marched two-abreast right down the rail line in full view of the amazed Marines. Weapons Company trained their heavy, 50.cal. Machine guns and B.A.R.'s on the Red's column and their deadly fire soon decimated thc Chinese. As frantic survivors scrambled over their dead and wounded comrades, Marine riflemen began to methodically pick off the remnants as if “Snapping In” on the rifle range.

All-in-all this 'first ever' clash between U.S. Marines and Red China's armed forces was not only a historic meeting but also validated the Marine Corps' ability to blend their regulars with newly-called up reservists and utilize their discipline, training, staunch leadership and historic- *elan* for victory.

Chapter 5
The "Yankee Clipper"

Waking to daylight I found myself safely abed in the 1st Marine Division Hospital in Hungnam North Korea. Now, probably November 3rd or 4th, my room held four or five other wounded if I remember correctly. Then and for some days I was only conscious and alert intermittently. Don't think I had regular meals for some time. Speaking of meals, breakfast is an interesting memory. We had small, individual boxes of dry cereal that you opened and poured milk into their waxed paper insides. Good old Cornflakes – almost like home. Right!

The three slugs that had ripped into me had fortunately passed through my lower side and arm missing bone or organs. The exit wound in my back had left a large, gaping wound. A Navy surgeon rather than stitching the wound, left it to drain covered with gauze bandages for weeks.

The weeks passed slowly into December mostly sleeping. During that time we heard scuttlebutt that "Chesty Puller" and a Marine unit entrained north had been ambushed by Red Chinese forces. The rumor turned out to be false as is the case with most war zone rumors. What actually happened was that a large Chinese force ambushed and surrounded a relief column (not "Chesty's") from Koto-ri headed north to aid the Marine Hagaru garrison about 15 miles or so north.

Tank-led leading units did manage to break out of the trap and make it to Hagaru after a vicious firefight. Included was a company of British Commandos with Col. Douglas Drysdale commanding. The British considered their commandos similar to America's Marine Corps. Talk about sharp, these Brit commandos dressed smartly, kept clean-shaven, even wearing their berets while in action.

Fighting valiantly for quite some time--the balance of the relief column finally ran out of ammo and were reluctantly forced to surrender.

Sometime in December, our hospital room had an unexpected and unusual pair of visitors. One afternoon two tall figures clad in heavy parkas and fur caps appeared. The famous baseball icon and New York Yankee superstar, Joe DiMaggio, known as the 'Yankee Clipper' was at my bedside. Wow! Right in the middle of a "Hot War"; I couldn't believe my eyes. As a rabid baseball fan and admirer of DiMaggio, his appearance was a Korean War memory I'd never forget. Joe was accompanied by "Lefty" O'Doul, a baseball star in his own right and DiMaggio's friend and mentor going back to their San Francisco ball-playing days. Right here in North Korea and not too far from action, Joe and 'Lefty' were braving the bone-chilling North Korea winter to visit and cheer up American hospitalized military. This unselfish act greatly enhanced my admiration for Joe. I also knew that in the pantheon\of Yankee greats only the 'Babe' ranked higher.

Asking how I felt, Joe handed me an authentic American League baseball autographed with his distinctive signature. Turning the ball over it read: "To Stanley, best wishes – Joe DiMaggio" Overwhelmed, all I could do was murmur "Gee. Thanks Joe." After DiMaggio and O'Doul left, still not ambulatory, I gave the ball to our room corpsman to mail home for me to Pittsburgh. Big mistake! When I returned home some months later I learned that my wonderful trophy never arrived: What a disappointment! It probably was either stolen or lost in the wartime mail. As rabid baseball fans would understand, the loss bothered me for years after Korea. Having this uplifting experience in the midst of war and then the loss, I'm sure you can understand my feelings.

Some days after the memorable visit, our room corpsman gave me a robe telling me to try some walking for the first time out in the hallway. Still vivid in my Korean memories, I found the hallway crowded with dozens of litter-bound wounded Red Chinese. Just after a few steps trying to walk I suddenly passed out. The fall somehow didn't cause any injuries, but back to bed. My return to bed didn't last very long. With casualties mounting from the late November and early December Reservoir actions our hospital needed more beds than were available. Soon I found myself and other wounded Marines being loaded onto transport planes and flown to Japan.

The evacuation took us to Japan's Yokuska Naval Hospital. Our stay was brief, one or two days. It was an interesting experience in that upon arriving, my beard and mustache were shaved by a Japanese nurse -a cutie. Only just five years from the end of WW II, being cared for and shaved by a recent enemy, now kind and good-natured. Again, with Chosin casualties arriving, many with frost-bite anguishing hands and feet, hospital facilities were at a premium. Our Navy Surgeons began to check us carefully to determine which needed to stay and which to evacuate back to the States.

Being one of those chosen for evacuation to the States, my litter was loaded into a C47 transport plane. We landed late that night or early morning for refueling at either Wake Island or Midway. We were too tired and sleepy to ask. The next day around 2 p.m., we passed over a beautiful sight – the California Coastline! Felt very elated and comforted that Korea was behind me and to be safely back home.

The plane's speaker began to broadcast the Los Angeles Ram's NFL game, making us feel really at home. Being a big sports fan since 1944 I was very familiar with the NFL, the Rams, and their famous players; quarterback Bob Waterfield, former Army All-American Glen Davis, and others.

After landing in California we were driven to Oak Knoll Naval Hospital in Oakland – now evening.

Our stay at Oak Knoll was again very short and soon we were on our way to the Philadelphia Navy Yard Hospital. Our military were making an effort to fly our war wounded to a hospital near their home as much as possible. With all this transferring going on I hadn't kept track of the calendar days. Just knew that it was probably late December. Arriving at the hospital and being assigned to a ward, it hit me. After inquiring with a nurse I learned that it was actually December 25th – Christmas Day! Missing the usual Christmas Eve Midnight Mass, celebrations and gift-giving didn't bother me, just happy to be back safely in Pennsylvania not far from my Pittsburgh home. I couldn't ask for a better Christmas gift than to be back home again – and recovering.

After changing into fresh pajamas and robe I felt well enough to walk my large ward area. While resting, the radio speaker played a recording new to me. "*Oh Mine Papa*" by an emerging star, Eddie Fisher. That evening and night passed contentedly sleeping well for the first time in a while. The next afternoon, a Navy surgeon's exam found my condition recovered enough for a 30-day R&R leave.

The next day, clad in my new 'winter greens' uniform I entrained for home. Talk about a mix-up! On arrival in Pittsburgh at my Aunt Marie's home she told me that my dad and stepmother were driving to the Philadelphia Hospital not knowing my situation. Ultimately they returned from Philly, somewhat upset, and took me home. Not having gotten along with my stepmother and not very close to dad – no brass band so to speak – or very much in the way of deep conversation. They were still disgruntled.

The 30-day leave went rather quickly. I met a girl that I would marry after return to duty. I also visited my Aunt Frances before leaving for Quantico, Virginia, my new duty station. She told me of a startling event. Aunt Frances, my dad's sister, had taken my younger brother and I to live with her family after my mother died of pneumonia. I was nine at the time, my brother Ron three.

Aunt Francis had a son and daughter, Junior and Marion, both being away at the time of my visit. During our get-together and conversation she related a startling psychic phenomena that occurred.

She told me how her daughter Marion had awakened in early November with disturbing pains in her side. Aunt Francis examined her for any signs of injury or possible skin damage as the pains persisted. She found no visible evidence of injury. The pains abated shortly, as abruptly as they had begun.

Aunt Francis further startled me saying; "Stanley, in talking to your Dad about Marion's painful experience and when it happened, we began to realize that they had occurred close to the time of your wounding!" Allowing for time and distance of course; they were now certain that Marion had definitely experienced a psychic phenomena.

I was taken aback somewhat having never devoted much thought to psychic events before. But it now brought to mind the movie “The Corsican Brothers” with Douglas Fairbanks Jr. Fairbanks played Siamese twins separated at birth and living far apart in two different countries. As adults when one would suffer a painful experience the other also felt the discomfort. Makes one think doesn't it?

Soon after learning of the unusual psychic event, I returned to duty. My orders sent me to the MCAS (Marine Corps Air Station) at Quantico, Virginia with duties as a radio operator in the base radio room. My exciting and perilous four-year enlistment ended in June of 1952 with an Honorable Discharge. Not before learning of another somber and saddening Korean event. I happened to meet a Marine, who was in Graves Registration detail. As a Marine boxer, one of the KIA's he handled and knew was a boxing heavyweight, Joe Coomer, killed with a round between the eyes. I remembered seeing Coomer in a Marine “smoker' boxing match at Cherry Point, North Carolina. The featured match was a heavy-weight match with Joe Coomer.

Closure

Forward to a sultry L.A. Summer in 1991, now a 39-year civilian after Korea and Honorable Discharge. The loss of the DiMaggio baseball would still caused regrets over the years as the “Clipper” would be in the news from time to time. His marriage to Marilyn Monroe was prominent, then his devotion to her memory as he placed flowers on her gravesite every year of their anniversary.

The much-valued baseball and its loss seemed to be another layer of depression added to the other somber and regretful Korean War memories. My wife, Roulti, knew the story of the “lost trophy” I had referred to it over the years and she realized how much it troubled me.

Near my birthday in July of 1991 I checked the mail, finding a few letters, a bill and a small, square box. Curious, I turned it over to find that it bore the return address of the Oakland Athletics Baseball Club. Wondering what it could be, I eagerly opened the intriguing package. It held an authentic American League baseball.

Turning the ball over, autographed words read: *"To Stanley a replacement – Best Wishes, Joe DiMaggio"* Wow! After 41 years – what a birthday present!

Happily showing the prized ball to my wife, she smiled with a "knowing" grin admitting that it was her doing. A week earlier I had mentioned to her that DiMaggio was to be honored at an A's game celebrating his 56-game hitting streak in 1941 -A record still intact. Remembering the "lost ball" story and unknown to me, she had phoned the Oakland A's offices and spoke to General Mgr. Sandy Alderson. As it turned out Alderson was also a former Marine so that coincidence along with my wife's feminine persuasion struck a responsive chord with Alderson – and DiMaggio.

The treasured memento represents a happy closure to a long-ago disappointment and now bears an honored niche in our home. We have a time-honored saying in the Corps: *Once a Marine, always a Marine.* It certainly rang true with Sandy Alderson – *Semper Fi* Sandy!

Chapter 6

Winters *and* Summers of Discontent

Now 1952 and married, I just couldn't seem to adjust comfortably to civilian life and marriage. Although I had buried conscious thoughts and memories of Korea, preferring not to think of war, something dark and disturbing was building within my psyche. Why this discontent and discomfort with civilian life; why this discomfort with married life; why this morose unhappiness without a discernible reason. Depression, melancholia and an aversion to social activities cropped up. Just didn't feel right in social gatherings. It seems my pre-war personality and outlook on life had been altered drastically and I didn't know why. In retrospect I feel that subconsciously I may have been recalling the visceral excitement of combat and unconsciously seeking combat's excitement and adrenalin rush.

By 1953 nagging discontent with civilian life, marriage and the dull 9 to 5 office work environment with dead-end jobs going nowhere seemed to strangle like a too-tight mental corset. Memories of pleasant visits to aunts, uncles and cousins years ago prompted a second marriage and a move to Cleveland, Ohio in 1954. Once again a nagging discomfort with jobs going nowhere led to more job changes and an increasing dislike for Cleveland's harsh weather and boring environment. Within five years the "Greener Pastures" began calling again culminating in a move to the sunny clime of Southern California and Los Angeles. Remembering the warm, sunny weather of Southern California from my 1948 Radio School days at Camp Del Mar, a move there seemed to promise a welcome change and a more comfortable and happy lifestyle. I hoped that "Old devil gloom" would cease to keep knocking at my mental equilibrium.

A short period of relative contentment passed. After a few years however the life-disturbing pattern of the past reappeared. Something was again nagging and interfering with attempts at a wholesome and successful career and marriage. Somehow I still didn't connect this pervasive uneasiness and discontent with work and marriage to the Korean War and the traumatic experience.

1979 found restlessness again calling. Remembering the charm and beauty of the San Francisco Bay Area and the striking Golden Gate Bridge, having visited there a few times, I decided to divorce and headed to northern California. Once there, I started my life over again in Sausalito, a charming tourist community nestled at the northern base of the Golden Gate Bridge with the shimmering landscape of San Francisco as a backdrop. One would think that eventually all these moves and changes would result in a calm and somewhat agreeable lifestyle. After less than a year in the Bay Area I married in 1980 with some so-so years to follow. But once again, even this cinematic setting became trumped by the realities of life. Marital and social uneasiness with a dash of melancholia again returned to disrupt my life of happiness.

In 1985 I learned of a reunion of the "Chosin Few" as the survivors of the vicious Chosin Reservoir Campaign were dubbed. Being held in San Diego, not far from Los Angeles,I decided to attend. I hoped to run into some of my *Anglico* comrades to learn of their experiences after I lost contact, when evacuated from the Sudong-ni battlefield and eventually to the States. Unexpectedly, the reunion and events there would lead to a huge impact on my mental health, ultimately causing the mind-shaking onset of P.T.S.D. or *Post-Traumatic Stress Disorder.*

During the first evening's get-together I didn't find any of my *Anglico* comrades but did meet Capt. Ed Stamford, one of our Anglico officers at Camp Lejeune. Stamford lead a close-air support spotting team during the Chosin Campaign attached to an Army unit on the East side of the Reservoir. Sadly, I learned that two of his radiomen, Bud Smith from Nebraska and Texan Billy Johnson were both killed when the Army battalion was badly mauled and practically destroyed by a Red Chinese Division. Before my discharge in 1952 I had heard that Smith and Johnson were missing at the Chosin, but now Stamford confirmed their deaths. Stamford himself barely made it back to Marine lines after a brief capture and a hectic, Injury-ridden escape from the Red Chinese.

I remembered Stamford from our Camp Lejeune *Anglico* days, but he had undergone quite a change. Back then he was rather stocky with brownish hair. Now his hair had whitened completely and he was much thinner in frame. Though not in my naval gunfire spotting team I had occasional contact with Smith and Johnson during our previous Hawaii and Viequez exercises in 1949. Both were good -natured decent kids, especially Smitty who seemed to be always in good humor and smiling. Sadly, Smitty would never again be riding broncos back home in Omaha, and Billy, the lanky, taciturn kid from Texas would never again enjoy a Red River sunset. Why?

The somber news also brought to mind that long-buried Sudong Valley's traumatic wounding followed by the *Last Rites* of the Church. Also brought to mind was the death of our team Sergeant and the severe wounding of our team officer during the same night's action. I only learned of their traumas right before my Honorable Discharge in 1952. It seems for some reason they had both gone up into the hills to spend the night with a rifle company. When the Chinese *Double Envelopment* hit that night they were overrun and shot by the flooding Chinese infantry.

Though they had taken command of our team shortly before sailing from San Diego for Korea that monumental September, we didn't have much time to get to know them well. The sad news of their dire consequences must have disturbed me to the point that I buried their names in my psyche. Even to this day, not remembering their names, even with doing some research, haunts me as if I was dishonoring their memory.

At the next evening's meeting just prior to dinner I was introduced to a black-garbed somber Chaplain. Not just *any* Chaplain, but Father Cornelius, "Connie" Griffin our regimental Chaplain who had performed the *Last Rites* over me that dark and traumatic night so long ago. What an unexpected and thrilling meeting! We shook hands as I thanked him for his care and words that dark, traumatic night on the Sudong battlefield. Father Griffin didn't say much and his deep-set eyes seemed to have a haunted look about them. I'm sure that the reunion had brought back many, many disturbing memories of North Korea and of his bleak experiences at the Chosin during the breakout.

Father Griffin's facial features were somewhat emaciated and scarred with his formerly dark hair now graying. I learned later that his cheek and jaw were hit with rounds from Chinese machine guns and that his assistant was killed instantly. Though Chaplain Griffin and his assistant were aiding and comforting wounded Marines in a panel truck with large Red Cross symbols on both sides, it didn't matter to the Chinese gunners. This deadly and uncalled-for event came during the Division's heroic breakout from the Chosin Reservoir trap. They had to fight through thousands of surrounding Red Chinese infantry on the road back and in the swarming hills above. It's been chronicles that elements of eight to ten Chincsc infantry divisions were involved in surrounding and attempting to annihilate the 1st Marine Division, the Red Chinese leader's ultimate political goal.

Thanks to Marine General O.P. Smith's leadership along with veteran combat officers and NCO's fighting spirit and bravery, the Division fought their way out gallantly. The Chosin breakout and tactics have been compared to Xenophon and his immortal Ten Thousand when they cut their way through Asiatic hordes to the Black Sea in the year 401 B.C.

Gen. Smith is also reputed to have refused X Corps Commander, Army Gen. Almond who advised that the Marine Division be evacuated by air from Hagaru-ri at the reservoir. Smith refused to lose any of his valuable equipment and supplies to the Chinese. In fact, the Marines also made sure that none of their wounded was left behind even bringing out as many of their dead as was possible with some being lashed to the barrels of artillery guns and hoods of vehicles.

Upon the conclusion of the mind-disturbing reunion I returned to the San Francisco Bay area, and home, not particularly expecting any mental repercussions from the reunion. I determined to put aside any intrusive thoughts or memories of Korea. Not long afterwards however, a gradual lack of concentration or career drive began to occur. In addition a troubling anger emerged as I had learned at the reunion that over 8100 of our MIA's (missing in action) in Korea were abandoned after the war's conclusion in 1953. I felt that President Truman and the Washington establishment had cowardly left our MIA's to wither and die in the hands of the barbarous North Koreans and Red Chinese. With the figure of over 8100 MIA's, it was a larger amount missing than after any previous war, even WWII. Inbred in all Marines is a love and a pride in the Corps and an almost brotherly love for comrades that engenders sorrow in us any time we learn of a friend or comrade being KIA or MIA.

VA Mental health clinicians counseling war veterans say that the veteran often agrees to a feeling as though there is a cemetery within their soul. They feel an overweening responsibility that they must honor and not forget their lost dead comrades. They can be tortured with shame or remorse if they forget a name, a face, an event that involves a comrade. This I can agree with as I had previously mentioned how forgetting the names of our team's severely wounded officer and the death of our team sergeant had evoked shame and remorse even to this day – many years later.

Carrying the mentally-disturbing confirmation of comrades' deaths and the unexpected meeting at the reunion reminded me of a former combat nurse, Beth Marie Murphy, and of her post-war feelings. "I was only given a glimpse of the trauma that I had pushed down for over 25 years and then given the skills to supposedly "move on". But without uncovering the war and its somber memories that I had buried, I wasn't ready to "move on."

Not long afterwards a new intrusive thought pattern began to emerge. Driving in certain areas of Marin County in the S.F. Bay Area, during my sales calls, certain landscape configurations and features would trigger distinctive memories of similar Korean landscapes and experiences.

One of the most disturbing and similar were the hills dominating a small shopping center in Terra-Linda nestled in a tiny valley-like setting. The sharply-rising hills were a dead-ringer of the Sudong valley hills. On entering the area, Sudong Valley and its hills flooded my memory. The similarity was so intense that without a conscious effort on my part, Sudong took over my thoughts to the point that even the discordant blare of the Chinese bugles echoing hill-to-hill above were recalled vividly.

The experience was so intrusive and realistic that I was rendered immobile -thinking and remembering. Feeling unable to continue my business day I would just sit in my car with my mind taken hold of, caught up in dark and somber memories. I would then return home to brood, indeed a "hostage of the mind." Another disturbing and recurring trigger was a particular stretch of Hwy 101 north as you approach Terra Linda. Here, the Fwy rises and curves between hills bringing back remembrances of the North Korean road and hills leading to the Sudong Valley. Both of these disturbing locations and images would occur with no conscious attempt to recall on my part. Usually they would result in interrupting or ending my work day and return home. Of course my wife couldn't understand, not being aware of P.T.S.D. and its debilitating effects. She felt that I should be grateful to have survived traumatic life-threatening injuries and to be able to "put the experiences behind me." Easy to say! It became harder to not acknowledge that something dolorous from my war experiences was alive within, and now bleeding into my present life -without any conscious consent.

I would usually try to respond "that it's easy for you to say, you just don't understand." But we never could get anywhere. So I would often withdraw, finding it harder and harder to acknowledge that some demon from the Korean War was stirring within, interfering with my present life, disrupting my career, impacting negatively on our marriage – without my consent.

CPT Stamford leading his Tactical Air Spotting Team and other Marines.

Left to Right: Bud Smith, Schaffer and Billy Johnson, with an Asian Yak

Chapter 7
P.T.S.D!

1987 found my career still faltering. Occasional anger and depressive feelings began to take hold. Memories of the reunion's sad disclosures and the meeting with Chaplain Griffin would at times haunt my reveries. Various triggers would lead to mental intrusions that interfered with career productivity and peace of mind. Triggers would occur without any desire or provocation on my part. Memorial Days, Veterans Days, names, certain cities would evoke Korean experiences or events.

My direct sales career involved making sales calls in San Francisco's financial district. I would usually start my day meeting with George, a WW II Navy veteran at a coffee shop for conversation and reminiscences. After some weeks of our get-togethers, George surprised me one morning with an unexpected comment: "Stan, I've been doing some reading lately about P.T.S.D., which is *Post-Traumatic Stress Disorder.* I think you may be experiencing this disorder. Your constant anger about Korea MIA's and your grief over the loss of your comrades kind'a tipped me off that something was wrong." I had never heard of P.T.S.D. until then so was surprised at George's comment and take. He continued his opinion that P.T.S.D. was affecting me, especially when I admitted to symptoms of depression, grief and lack of concentration in my work. I mentioned also that these intrusions were even affecting marital amity.

A day or so later George convinced me that I may indeed be suffering the mental anguish of P.T.S.D., and suggested: "Why don't we go visit the DAV (Disabled American Veterans) about your symptoms and maybe get some help?" "I don't know George" I responded. I was feeling some ambivalence, somewhat unsure – probably my procrastination showing up. George told me that he had read of a "shrink" named Gabriel who wrote that: "In every war since WW I more vets have become psychiatric casualties than were killed in action." Having second thoughts I agreed to give it a try. The DAV offices were fortunately nearby downtown so I agreed to meet him the next day and try them.

Arriving at the DAV offices the next morning, we were interviewed by an understanding representative, who was himself a disabled war veteran. Listening to my Korean War experiences and the litany of the disruptive symptoms plaguing me, he agreed with George that I was probably suffering the onset of P.T.S.D.. "What can I do, where can I go to try and shake this problem?" I asked. He informed me that there was help available consisting of therapeutic counseling for war vets suffering with these symptoms. He related that I could probably get some help and comfort with an organization called "Vet Centers". He mentioned a Vet Center not too far from my residence in Marin County.

P.T.S.D SCREENING TEST

Have had nightmares of war or thought about it when not wanted?

Tried hard not to think about war or went out of your way to avoid situations that reminded you of war?

Were constantly on guard, watchful, easily startled? Felt detached from others, activities or your surroundings?

Being an inveterate procrastinator, I put off calling a Vet Center to think it over for a while. Sure enough the mental depredations continued its torment. At times a group of hills, a road, or certain configurations in nature would trigger reminders of Korea with troubling flashbacks; Memorial Day, Veterans Day was always certain to affect me negatively. If I attended these memorials P.T.S.D. effects would increase in intensity; on the other hand, by not attending these memorials I would feel ashamed and remorseful as if I had forgotten and dishonored my lost comrades—a mental quandary. Remembering my lost *Anglico* comrades, their young faces as I knew them would at times result in tears of grief, leading to self-recriminations of mental weakness. And being unmanly, I was in a mixed-up turmoil. What a disturbing situation.

After some time I finally decided to give the Vet Center a try and was given an appointment almost immediately at their nearby Marin County facilities. Although apprehensive and a little worried of the possible involvement in counseling therapy, I made the initial appointment on time.

The Vet Center offices consisted of a variety of rooms sized to allow for individual or group counseling activities. The Center was staffed with two veterans, Randy and Harold. I was introduced to Randy who would be my counselor. After a few minutes of discussion I felt a little more comfortable and less apprehensive learning that Randy was also a former Marine and Purple Heart recipient in Vietnam. His friendliness and understanding approach soon had me recounting My Korean War experiences and how I was now undergoing life-disturbing mental intrusions and their effects. Both being former Marines, we soon developed a comfortable rapport, trust and understanding.

Even though my first counseling session, when the grief aspect of my disturbances arose, it prompted some tears. With Randy's understanding and assurances that it was "OK" to feel the emotions of grief and sorrow when recalling lost comrades I felt a little more at ease. Randy further counseled that "You've buried your experience and feelings too long, and with your recent reunion and its somber information your subconscious feelings are now fighting to emerge."

The balance of the session was an encouragement to verbalize experiences, feelings and emotions that had apparently been festering for many years – and buried. "You've been burying your war experiences in your subconscious, a subconscious that didn't want to allow you to face them" Randy advised. Mentioning that I felt some shame and weakness in not being able to handle these mental intrusions and their disturbances alone, he assured me that my situation and its effects were quite common with war vets and not something to be ashamed of. At the end of the session with Randy, I agreed at his suggestion that we meet weekly for one-hour of counseling.

Weeks went by, then months with Randy's prompting to recall and understand my mental intrusions leading to an almost constant depressive, grief-ridden state of mind.

One particular trigger was that the beginning of every November with its overcast skies it would take me back to that deadly November 2nd and the ensuing traumas of long ago. Needless to say, this and other triggers and their impact wore negatively on my career and marital happiness .Other sure-fire triggers would be when Nebraska or Omaha were mentioned in the news. I would remember *Anglico* comrades Bud Smith, Billy Johnson, Bob fish and Ray Lemmons all KIA; and of course our spotting team Sergeant killed the same November 2nd. I especially remembered Bud Smith for his escapades attempting to ride a wild horse after our Viequez exercise. I suspect Smitty was a bit of a cowboy at heart as he couldn't resist trying to ride an Asian Yak in North Korea. I have a photo of Smitty and one of his team buddies sitting on a Yak so I guess he made it.

Ray Lemmons I remember from boot camp days, Ray was shot by a NKPA sniper during the Seoul street fighting .Ray was evacuated to a hospital ship but didn't make it back home to St. Louis. Ray and my best buddy Johnny were close friends growing up in St. Louis and enlisting in the Marines together.

Bud Smith and Billy Johnson were radiomen in Capt. Stamford's close-air support team. Stamford whom I mentioned earlier and his spotting team had been temporarily loaned out to an Army battalion unit driving up the east side of the Chosin Reservoir while the Marines were driving to the south and west of the Reservoir toward Hagaru which became Division HQ , then ultimately reaching as far as Yudam-ni, the farthest of the Division's penetration into desolate North Korea.

The Army unit Capt. Stamford's close-air team was supporting took a horrific mauling. Surrounded, cut off and practically destroyed as Red Chinese infantry division swarming by the thousands. Stamford and only a handful of Army escaped, many taking refuge across the icy arm of the Reservoir. Sadly, Smitty and Johnson were among the KIA's. Somehow Stamford somehow escaped during the combat's blackish gloom and was able to make it back to Marine lines near Hagaru.

A quote that seemed to me to be very appropriate for the recovery process no matter what the combat traumas are called was by Dr. Edward Tick, M.D.

"The healing and cleansing of mentally disturbed veterans commonly occur when we relive memories and their accompanying feelings so that they may be expressed and relieved just as shrapnel must make its way to the surface and be removed; similarly, traumatic events need a catharsis to enhance recovery."

Time passed as the debilitating effects continued. As ongoing therapy I spent a year of weekly counseling at the San Francisco DVA Hospital with an extremely kind and sensitive psychiatrist who recommended starting to take a medication along with current counseling sessions. Sometime later I returned to the Marin County Vet Center experiencing group and individual counseling. Months later with only gradual and sporadic improvement I was assigned to a kind, caring and experienced lady psychiatrists who soon changed the medications as we continued with semi-monthly sessions.

Once again I found my VA counselor very caring. In fact, this lady psychiatrist Dr. Keram was so sensitive that she could only work with troubled veterans part-time. Her feelings and sensibilities could only stand so much of her veteran clients anguish and horrific experiences without being mentally disturbed and saddened herself. Talk about empathy. What a wonderfully caring lady.

After being encouraged and spurred by my various counselors over the years, I began to try doing some freelance writing hoping to achieve publication success in magazines of varied genre. I also joined some writing classes with some encouraging improvement in style and ability to communicate. The writing activity began to help somewhat as the intensity and occurrences of P.T.S.D.'s intrusions seemed to diminish somewhat. Although business concentration and marital affairs were still not what they should be in a normal life situation, Ole'man "greener pastures" still called sporadically.

When mentioning thoughts of pulling up stakes and moving once again to my wife, it always would lead to anger and conflict. She was always dead set against moving. Two people each with a different outlook on life and living situations. As most troubled veterans will attest to, it was difficult for wives to understand an affected veteran and the mental vagaries of P.T.S.D. "Why can't you be happy that you survived war while many died?" was my wife's usual comment. This attitude never helped of course, it just amplified the frustration and regret of not being understood.

Understanding this and other dilemmas affecting veterans and wives or loved ones, the Vet Centers, V A Hospitals and clinics offer experienced family counseling as well when needed or requested. Unfortunately, despite valiant efforts by DVA clinicians, separations and divorce continue to be prevalent among troubled veterans. Having tried this family counseling myself, it never seemed to help us. Not enough understanding on either side I guess. Two people--looking at the same problem in a different light and pre-conditioned attitudes--made it difficult to affect marital amity.

By 2005, still on medications and occasional counseling therapy, I was able to concentrate somewhat better and made a dedicated effort to write on a more regular basis. Consistent discipline was still not there but I tried. My writing was primarily in the military genre for national military-oriented magazines with some articles published in various military publications.. This helped both my mental situation and provided a boost for my self-worth having accomplished something worthwhile – finally. Veterans and/or their loved ones reading this may consider the plan and method to offset P.T.S.D. by seeking some positive interest in their daily life. I realize that it's easy to say, but I would heartily suggest contacting your local DVA Clinic or Vet Center. I'm sure that they can analyze your situation and offer encouraging suggestions.

Chapter 8
Closure?

Combat sends the warrior on a post-war mission to make sense out of chance. P.T.S.D. is the struggle of the mind, body and spirit in that quest.
Dr. Emily Keram MD

Looking back over the years living with the mental incursions, intrusions and debilitating effects of P.T.S.D. it engenders a good deal of soul-searching: Soul-searching to make sense out of and attempting to understand P.T.S.D.'s root trauma and the resultant disruptive vagaries of the mind.

Attempting to understand and apply the many clinical solutions offered by such a variety of VA clinicians, as I have experienced, has proved to be quite a daunting task to say the least. Having engaged in VA counseling sessions for years – almost twenty years now – both individual and group counseling as have many mentally-troubled war veterans, I still find it difficult to realize why this malady has been so constant, so unrelenting for so long. The following quote by Lord Tennyson addresses this: *"Oh sorrow, wilt thou live with me as no casual mistress but as a wife."*

The mental chains of P.T.S.D. are usually ever-present although their dolorous effects can vary in intensity and occurrence. I still find it hard to fathom how P.T.S.D.'s mental intrusions can interrupt our normal daily thought processes – even without any cognitive intent on our part. Of course its usually the result of a variety of triggers; the unexpected triggers that usher in the disturbing and intrusive mental malady referred to as P.T.S.D. without our cognitive permission. Triggers can be varied and sundry; wartime experiences emerging, Veterans Day, Memorial Day, war movies, names and places of lost comrades, military reunions and others. You may say, why attend these memorials and reunions if it causes mental disruptions to emerge. As I mentioned earlier, it was a quandary for me to decide to go or not to go to these events as it is for many war veterans. It seems common to feel a need almost a duty to remember and honor our lost comrades--especially our lost buddies.

Within the past few years, still undergoing occasional counseling though the war-related mental intrusions have drastically diminished, a side-effect of P.T.S.D. has occurred. Due to the habit-forming effects of P.T.S.D. – in most cases – the habit of falling prey to depression, grief and general un-happiness can spread its somber tentacles to interfere with our marital and personal relationships. It has certainly been the case with me seemingly to shift the usual P.T.S.D. -related feelings of depression, grief and lethargy into my personal life, marriage and aspirations.

I fully believe in the habit-forming aspect of P.T.S.D. and its consequent mental disruptions. I'm sure that many veterans reading this may concur having suffered the identical habit-forming side-effects. It took me many years to understand and agree with this aspect of P.T.S.D. That's fine, now how to break this disturbing habit? As William Shakespeare once put it; "Aye, that's the rub."

As I understand it talking to VA clinicians, the first step to breaking this dolorous habit is to understand that these intrusive thoughts, in many cases, are habits accumulated over the years rather than the product of cognitive thinking. My recent, much-valued Vet Center counselor, Mr. Bill Dolon, has been a veritable fountain of helpful ideas and suggestions. One in particular that I hadn't ever considered was to try to look upon P.T.S.D. and its dolorous effects as "Another part of life and try to accept it as such," What I try to do to defy and lessen the effects of this habit is this: At times when a mental intrusion occurs 'Out of the blue' so to speak, I first try to force myself to be aware that an intrusion of habit is occurring. This is not always as easy as the intrusive event may take hold quickly and before cognitive thinking can kick in.

Here are some step-by-step suggestions for my readers:

1. **Make yourself aware that a 'Habit Intrusion' is forming.**

2. **Ask yourself 'Why' at this time**
3. **Try to relate the intrusion to similar ones to determine if it's part of a 'Pattern'.**
4. **After realizing the 'Why' and 'Pattern' try to put the intrusive event into a cognitive thought process to interrupt the forming habit.**

Of course realizing that you're in the throes of a mentally-disruptive habit is your first step in combating and interrupting the habit. I'm currently trying to apply my own 4-step formula to curb my habitual mental intrusions. It's too soon to draw any definitive conclusion but I feel that the formula holds some prom ise of success. I certainly hope that it helps and comforts my veteran comrades of all wars reading this having their own ongoing struggles with P.T.S.D.

My suggested formula being only the first step facing our mental incursions affecting mind, body and spirit, could at least be a start in our curative efforts. I agree 100% with the premise of Dr. Keram; "Yes, it's more than just a mental joust, it does indeed affect one's mind, body and spirit."

In conversing with my current VA counselor, he seems to urge a second step in pursuing the long-sought recovery from P.T.S.D. and its depressions, grief and melancholia. He counsels that an extremely helpful tactic would be to look at our traumatic experiences and resultant mental incursions not as an insurmount-able malady but one that can eventually be controlled with time and effort. Yes, even though unwanted or unexpected, still a part of life. It certainly was and is a part of my life and many other veterans; the trauma of combat and the onset of P.T.S.D. and its mental intrusions but surely not a common occurrence during one's lifetime.

I must say though, and you may agree, at the least this premise is worth thinking about and considering as we struggle to seek and find a salutary solution to P.T.S.D.'s disruptive events on the veteran, our spouses, and on our loved ones.

The more I consider the premise of 'Habit' and trying to look upon the depredations of P.T.S.D. as 'Just part of life', the more I'm prone to agree that it may eventually contribute to diminishing the somber effects of the malady – if I can just stay with it! To combat veterans suffering with this mental plague, please, GIVE IT A TRY!

As to the "Pattern" aspect of P.T.S.D. in relation to our thinking that the intrusions and disturbances must be accepted as just a part of life I somewhat agree. The difficulty in accepting this premise is that yes, it has been a pattern, and yes, it can be looked upon as just a part of life; however this over-looks the usual lack of cognitive thinking and input in the process. Never, in all these years of suffering with the effects of P.T.S.D. has there been a disruptive incident due to cognitive thinking. Almost Every incident that I can remember has been due to some sort of trigger, causing a mental problem.

Now, in this regard it seems to me that we may try to intervene in this dolorous pattern of triggers bringing on an incident of P.T.S.D. Possibly, if we can recognize that a trigger is occurring <u>before</u> it becomes a full-blown mental or physical intrusion would we not then have a darn good chance of lessening, even interrupting or stopping the incident--easy to say. Yes, easy to say but have we not used mind discipline and cognitive thinking to curb emotions such as hate, envy, anger and happiness during events in our daily lives. If we can successfully recognize and interrupt the triggering and patterns we can then possibly begin our mental "comeback" by going on to ask ourselves the "Why" and indulge in an in-depth examination of the "Pattern" aspect. With all this dedicated positive ruminations I would think that by then the original triggering and pattern would be sufficiently lessened.

If this formula does prove to be helpful in some manner perhaps we can go on to examine in depth the individual harmful effects of P.T.S.D. such as grief, depression, melancholia, etc. I've been encouraged by a variety of clinicians specializing in P.T.S.D. and its mental effects that a little plumbing of one's mind and soul can do no harm and may in fact prove to be constructive. Just the interruption of the trigger and patterns in a thoughtful manner could and may help immeasurably. Surely something to think about and to be considered--agreed?

Considering the triggers and patterns of one's P.T.S.D. intrusions leading to depression, grief and melancholia mentioned,

I'd like to touch on another disruptive side-effect. I've suffered this side-effect as have many thousands of P.T.S.D.-laden veterans have. It's the inability to concentrate on our jobs and workaday careers. Lack of concentration as you can well understand is completely incompatible with achieving career success – any career. Being involved in direct sales, lack of concentration was insidious, seemingly struggling for supremacy with P.T.S.D.'s many other debilitating effects. Unlike the usual triggers and patterns of P.T.S.D.'s intrusions, lack of concentration was not as obvious and recognizable at first. Only obvious when realizing at the end of a given work day that nothing positive in sales was achieved due to lack of concentration. Many a day I would attribute lack of sales success to tiredness or bleak, cold weather overlooking my lack of discipline and drive. We can only fool ourselves for so long, can't we? As one would expect sales volume was beginning to recede along with income. Eventually this income fall-off led to marital strife.

Shame at allowing this lack of drive and discipline to occur along with my wife's natural displeasure with the drop in income understandably led to almost constant arguments and anger between us. One saving factor that helped us financially was my monthly disability payment from the VA--having applied for disability with the VA some years earlier

Lack of concentration as you can well understand is completely incompatible with achieving career success – any career. Being involved in direct sales, lack of concentration was insidious, seemingly struggling for supremacy with P.T.S.D.'s many other debilitating effects. Unlike the usual triggers and patterns of mental intrusions, lack of concentration was not as obvious or recognizable at first. It only became obvious when realizing at the end of a given work day that nothing positive in my sales efforts was achieved due to this concentration problem. Many a day I would attribute lack of sales success to tiredness, or bleak, cold weather, overlooking or not wanting to face my lack of concentration. We can only fool ourselves for so long, can't we? As one would expect, sales volume was receding along with income, the fall-off leading to marital strife.

Shame began to creep in at allowing this lack of drive and

discipline to occur along with my wife's natural displeasure with the dwindling income, understandably led to arguments and anger between us.

One saving factor that helped us financially was my monthly disability payment from the DVA. Having applied for military-based disability some years earlier, I was now compensated for the three in-and-out bullets along with an additional allowance for the ongoing P.T.S.D. disruptions. To my veteran comrades reading this, don't hesitate to apply for any compensation that you feel you may have earned. Don't be ashamed to apply if you feel that you're honestly deserving of a disability award. Remember, this compensation has been voted in overwhelmingly in Congress in appreciation of our service and war-incurred physical and mental sufferings.

If one feels deserving of disability compensation you can apply to your local Vet Center. Their experienced and caring staff – veterans themselves, are prepared and happy to aid deserving vets. The book's comprehensive glossary provides Vet Center locations, addresses and telephone numbers Nationwide. I would highly recommend this step. For me it was the beginning of my journey for relief and some semblance of closure. One mistake I made was not realizing that I had disability compensation available and deserving for my wartime traumatic wounds. Not until thirty years after my Honorable Discharge did I learn of the benefits available.

As I write this it's now the year 2011 and I find that my P.T.S.D. intrusions and disruptions have diminished greatly, allowing me the introspective ability to step back – figuratively and to finally fully realize and understand the ramifications of P.T.S.D. I sincerely hope that my journey through war's trauma and the 20-plus years of mental incursions and debilitating effects that I've related help in some way to alert and to provide guidance for my fellow veterans and their loved ones as they share the rigors of P.T.S.D.

To reiterate: remember that this dolorous malady is <u>not</u> completely curable, but can be managed, as we've been advised by experienced VA mental clinicians in this field. That being said, you need take heart and allow yourself to let a cognitive thought process become an ally and consider the 4-step formula mentioned previously. Many troubled veterans, myself included, have been seriously relieved and comforted to the point that they've achieved results of almost complete closure.

Another often-needed service is that the Vet Centers can also provide the troubled veteran and his family or loved one, family counseling. In many documented cases forestalling breakups and divorce that can be especially detrimental to children currently undergoing the rigors of P.T.S.D.

Addendum

In addition to the hundreds of Vet Centers available all across our Nation, VA Hospitals and out-patient clinics also provide P.T.S.D. counseling. They also offer trained clinicians with the expertise and experience to aid the P.T.S.D.-laden veteran. In addition, both Vet Centers and VA outpatient clinics offer family counseling to the veteran and his loved ones. In many cases preventing breakup or divorces that we know is especially detrimental where children are involved.

It takes some time between your original application and any compensation awarded. Don't be ashamed to apply if you feel that you're honestly deserving of any disability award. Remember, disability compensation has been voted in overwhelmingly in appreciation of our service and post-war mental and physical tribulations stemming from our military experiences and traumas.

The more I consider my counselor's premises of “Habit” and trying to look upon the depredations of P.T.S.D. as “Just a part of life” the more I'm prone to agree that it will eventually help a great deal in diminishing the somber effects of the malady if I can just stay with it! To my veteran comrades reading this, please GIVE IT A TRY!

Appendix

Medal of Honor recipients
Korean War (1950 – 1953)
U.S. Marine Corps

*Abrell, Charles G., Co. E, 2nd Bn, Jun 10, 1951, The Punchbowl
Cpl. USMC, 1st Marines

Barber, William E., Co F, 2nd Bn, Nov.28-Dec.2, Toktong Pass
Capt. USMC, 7th Marines, 1950

*Baugh, William B., Co G, 3rd Bn, Nov. 29, 1950, Near Koto-ri
Pfc. USMC, 1st Marines

Cafferata, Hector A., Co F, 2nd Bn, Nov. 28, 1950, Toktong Pass
Pvt, USMC, 7th Marines

*Champagne, David B., Co A, 1st Bn, May 28,1952, near Panmun-jon, Cpl. USMC, 7th Marines

*Christianson, Stanley R. Co E, 2nd Bn, Sept. 29, 1950, Seoul, Pfc. USMC, 1st Marines

Commiskey, Henry A., Co C, 1st Bn, Sept. 20, 1950, Yungdungp'o
2Lt., USMC, 1st Marines

*Davenport, Jack A., Co G, 3rd Bn, Sept. 21, 1951, Songnae-dong
Cpl. USMC, 5th Marines

Davis, Raymond G., 1st Bn, C.O., Dec1-4 1950, near Yudam-ni
Lt.Col USMC, 7th Marines

Dewey, Duane E, Co E 2nd Bn, Apr 16, 1952near Panmunjon
Cpl. USMC, 5th Marines

*Garcia, Fernando L., Co I,3rd Bn, Sept. 5,1952, Bunker Hill
PFC USMC, 5th Marines

*Gomez, Edward, Co E, 2nd Bn, Sept. 14, 1951, the Punchbowl
PFC USMC, 1st Marines

*Guillen, Ambrosio, Co F, 2nd Bn, July 25, 1953, near Panmunjon
Ssgt, USMC, 7th Marines

*Johnson, James E., Co J 3rd Bn, Dec. 2, 1950, Yudam-ni
Sgt. USMC, 7th Marines

*Kelly, John D., Co C. 1st Bn, May 28, 1952 near Panmunjon
Pfc USMC, 7th Marines

*Kelso, Jack W., Co I, 3rd Bn, Oct. 2, 1952, Detroit Hill
Pfc USMC, 7th Marines

Kennemore, Robert, Co E, 2n d Bn, Nov27/28 1950, Yudam-ni
Ssgt USMC, 7th Marines

*Littleton, Herbert, Co C, 1st Bn, Apr. 22, 1951, Chunchon
Pfc USMC, 7th Marines

*Lopez, Baldomero, Co A, 1st Bn, Sept. 15, 1950, Inchon
1Lt. USMC, 5th Marines

*Mathews, Daniel P., Co F, 2nd Bn, Mar. 28 1953, Vegas Hill
Sgt USMC, 7th Marines

*Mausert, Frederick, Co B, 1st Bn, Sept. 12, 1951, the Punchbowl
Sgt USMC, 7th Marines

McLaughlin, Alford L., Co L, 3rd Bn Sept 4-5,1952, Bunker Hill
Pfc USMC, 5th Marines

*Mitchell, Frank N., Co A, 1st Bn, Nov. 26, 1950, near Yudam-ni

1Lt. USMC, 7th Marines

*Monegan, Walter C., Co F, 2nd Bn, Sep 17-20,1950, near Sosa-ri
Pfc USMC, 1st Marines

*Moreland, Whitt L., Co C 1st Bn, May 29, 1951, Kwaghi-dong
Pfc USMC, 5th Marines

Murphy, Raymond G., Co A, 1st Bn, Feb. 3, 1953, Pan munjon
2Lt. USMC, 5th Marines

Myers, Reginald R., 3rd Bn, Nov. 29, 1950, Hagaru-ri
Maj, USMC, 1st Marines

*Obregon, Eugene A., Co G, 3rd BN, Sept. 26, 1950, Seoul
Pfc USMC, 5th Marines

O'Brien, George H,, Co. H 3rd Bn, Oct. 27, 1952, Panmunjon,
2Lt. USMC, 7th Marines

*Phillips, Lee H., Co E 2nd Bn, Nov. 4, 1950, Sudong
Cpl. USMC, 7th Marines

*Poynter, James I., Co. A 1st Bn, Nov. 4, 1950, Sudong
Sgt. USMC, 7th Marines

*Ramer, George H., Co I, 3rd Bn, Sept. 12,1951, Punchbowl
2Lt. USMC, 7th Marines

*Reem, Robert D., Co H 3rd Bn, Nov. 6, 1950, Chinhung-ni
2Lt. USMC, 7th Marines

*Shuck, William E., Co. G 3rd Bn, July 3, 1952, Bunker Hill
Ssgt USMC, 7th Marines

Simanek, Robert E., Co F 2nd Bn, Aug. 17, 1952, Bunker Hill
Pfc USMC, 5th Marines

Sitter, Carl L., Co. G 3rd Bn, Nov.29/30 1950, Hagaru-ri
Capt. USMC, 1st Marines

*Skinner, Sherrod, Batty.F 2nd Bn, Oct. 26, 1952, Panmunjon,
2Lt. USMC, 11th Marines

Van Winkle, Archie, Co. B, 1stBn, Nov. 2, 1950, Sudong
Ssgt USMC, 7th Marines

*Vittori, Joseph, Co F 2nd Bn, Sept.15/16 1951, Punchbowl
Cpl USMC, 1st Marines

*Watkins, Lewis G., Co I 3rd Bn, Oct. 7, 1952, Detroit Hill
Ssgt USMC, 7th Marines

Wilson, Harold E., Co G 3rd Bn, Apr. 23/24, 1951, near Chunchon
Tsgt USMC, 1st Marines

*Windrich, William, Co I 3rd Bn, Dec. 1, 1950, Yudam-ni
Ssgt USMC, 5th Marines

*Posthumous Award

VET CENTERS

ALASKA

Anchorage Vet Center 4201 Tudor Centre Drive Suite 115
Anchorage AK 99508 (907) 563-6966

Fairbanks Vet Center 540 4th Ave., Suite 100 Fairbanks AK 99701
(907) 456-4238

Kenai Vet Center
43335 Kalifornsky Beach Rd. #4 Bldg. F, Suite 4 Red Diamond Ctr
Soldotna AK 99669 (907) 260-7640

Wasilla Vet Center
851 E. West Point Drive Suite 111
Wasilla AK 99654 (907)376-4318

ALABAMA

Birmingham Vet Center
1201 2nd Avenue South Birmingham AL 35233 (205)212-3122

Mobile Vet Center
2577 Government Blvd. Mobile AL 36606 (251) 478-5906

Montgomery Vet Center 4405 Atlanta Highway Montgomery AL
36109 (334) 273-7796

ARKANSAS

Fayetteville Vet Center
1416 N. College Ave. Fayetteville AR 72703
(479)582-7152

Little Rock Vet Center
201 W. Broadway St., Suite A North Little Rock AR 72114 (501)
324-6395

ARIZONA

Phoenix East Valley Vet Center

1303 S Longmore, Suite #5 Mesa AZ 85202
(480)610-6727

Phoenix Vet Center
77 E. Weldon, Suite 100 Phoenix AZ 85012 (602) 640-2981

Prescott Vet Center
3180 Stillwater Drive, Suite A Prescott AZ 86305
(928) 778-3469

Tucson Vet Center
3055 N. First Avenue Tucson AZ 85719 (520) 882-0333

<u>CALIFORNIA</u>

Santa Cruz County Vet Center
1350 41st Ave, Suite 102 Capitola CA 95010 (831) 464-4575

Chico Vet Center
280 Cohasset Road, Suite 100 Chico CA 95926
(530) 899-8549

San Bernardino Vet Center
1325 E. Cooley Drive, Suite 101 Colton CA 92324 (909)801-5762

East Los Angeles Vet Center
5400 E. Olympic Blvd. #140 Commerce CA 90022 (323) 728-9966

Concord Vet Center
1899 Clayton Rd., Suite 140 Concord CA 94520 (925) 680-4526

Corona Vet Center
800 Magnolia Avenue, Suite 110 Corona CA 92879 (951) 734-0525

West Los Angeles Vet Center
5730 Uplander Way, Suite 100 Culver City CA 90230 (310) 641-0326

Redwoods Vet Center
2830 G Street, Suite A Eureka CA 95501 (707) 444-8271

Fresno Vet Center
3636 North 1st St., Suite 112
Fresno CA 93726

(559) 487-5660

Orange County Vet Center
12453 Lewis St., Suite 101 Garden Grove CA 92840 (714) 776-0161

Los Angeles Vet Center 1045 W. Redondo Beach Blvd. Suite 150 Gardena CA 90247 (310)767-1221

Modesto Vet Center
1219 N. Carpenter Road, Ste. 12 Modesto CA 95351 (209) 569-0713

Oakland Vet Center
1504 Franklin St., Suite 200 Oakland CA 94612 (510) 763-3904

Peninsula Vet Center 2946 Broadway St, Redwood City CA 94062 (650) 299-0672

Northbay Vet Center 6225 State Farm Drive Suite 101 Rohnert Park CA 94928 (707) 586-3295

Sacramento Vet Center
1111 Howe Avenue, Suite #390 Sacramento CA 95825 (916) 566-7430

San Diego Vet Center 2790 Truxtun Road, Ste. 130 San Diego CA 92106 (858) 624-1500

San Francisco Vet Center
505 Polk Street San Francisco CA 94102 (415)441-5051

San Jose Vet Center
278 North 2nd St. San Jose CA 95112 (408) 993-0729

San Marcos Vet Center
One Civic Center Dr., Suite 150 San Marcos CA 92069 (760) 744-6914

Sepulveda Vet Center 9737 Haskell Ave. Sepulveda CA 91343 (818) 892-9227

Ventura Vet Center

790 E. Santa Clara St., Suite 100 Ventura CA 93001 (805) 585-1860

COLORADO

Boulder Vet Center
2336 Canyon Blvd. Suite 103 Boulder CO 80302 (303) 440-7306

Colorado Springs Vet Center
416 E. Colorado Avenue Colorado Springs CO 80903 (719) 471-9992

Denver Vet Center
7465 East First Avenue, Suite B Denver CO 80230 (303) 326-0645

Fort Collins Vet Center 2509 Research Blvd. Ft. Collins CO 80526 (970)221-5176

Grand Junction Vet Center
2472 FRd., Unit #16 Grand Junction CO 81505 (970) 245-4156

CONNECTICUT

Danbury Vet Center
457 Main St Danbury CT 06831 (203) 798-8422

Norwich Vet Center
2 Cliff St. Norwich CT 06360 (860)887-1755

Hartford Vet Center
25 Elm Street, Suite A Rocky Hill CT 06067 (860) 563-8800

New Haven Vet Center 141 Captain Thomas Blvd. West Haven CT 06516 (203) 932-9899

WASHINGTON, DC

Washington Vet Center
1250 Taylor St, NW Washington DC 20011 (202) 726-5212

DELAWARE

Wilmington Vet Center
VAMC, Bldg 3 1601 Kirkwood Highway
Wilmington DE 19805 (302)994-1660

FLORIDA

Ft Myers Vet Center
4110 Center Pointe Dr Unit 204 Ft Myers FL 33916
(239) 479-4401

Fort Lauderdale Vet Center
713 NE 3rd Ave. Ft. Lauderdale FL 33304
(954) 356-7926

Gainesville Vet Center
105 N.W 75th Street, Suite 2 Gainesville FL 32607 (352)331-1408

Jacksonville Vet Center
300 East State St., Suite J Jacksonville FL 32202 (904) 232-3621

Palm Beach Vet Center
Spectrum Center 2311 10th Ave., N. #13 Lake Worth FL 33461
(561) 585-0441

Melbourne Vet Center 2098 Sarno Road Melbourne FL 32935
(321) 254-3410

Miami Vet Center
8280 NW 27th St., Suite 511 Miami FL 33122 (305) 718-3712

Orlando Vet Center
5575 S. Semoran Blvd. #36 Orlando FL 32822 (407) 857-2800

Pensacola Vet Center
4501 Twin Oaks Drive, Suite 104 Pensacola FL 32506 (850) 456-5886

Sarasota Vet Center
4801 Swift Rd., Suite A Sarasota FL 34231 (941) 927-8285

St. Petersburg Vet Center
2880 1st Ave. North St. Petersburg FL 33713 (727) 893-3791

Tallahassee Vet Center 548 Bradford Road Tallahassee FL 32303
(850) 942-8810

Tampa Vet Center
8900 N Armenia Ave. #312 Tampa FL 33604 (813) 228-2621

GEORGIA

Atlanta Vet Center 1440 Dutch Valley Place, Suite 1100, Box 55 Atlanta GA 30324 (404) 347-7264

North Atlanta Vet Center 930 River Centre Place Lawrenceville GA 30043 (770)963-1809

Macon Vet Center 750 Riverside Drive Macon GA 31201 (478)477-3813

Savannah Vet Center
308 A Commercial Dr Savannah GA 31406 (912) 652-4097

GUAM

Guam Vet Center
222 Chalan Santo Papa Reflection Ctr., Ste 201 HagatnaGU 96910 (671) 472-7160

HAWAII

Hilo Vet Center
126 Pu uhonu Way, Suite 2 Hilo HI 96720 (808) 969-3833

Honolulu Vet Center
1680 Kapiolani Blvd., Suite F-3 Honolulu HI 96814 (808) 973-8387

Kailua-Kona Vet Center
Hale Kui Plaza Suite 207 73-4976 Kamanu St. Kailua-Kona HI 96740 (808) 329-0574

Kauai Vet Center 3-3367 Kuhio Hwy. Ste #101 Lihue HI 96766 (808)246-1163-

Maui Vet Center 35 Lunalilo Street Suite #101 Wailuku HI 96793 (808) 242-8557

IOWA

Cedar Rapids Vet Center
1642 42nd Street NE Cedar Rapids IA 52402 (319) 378-0016

Des Moines Vet Center
2600 Martin Luther King PI Des Moines IA 50310 (515) 284-4929

Sioux City Vet Center

1551 Indian Hills Drive Suite 214
Sioux City IA 51104 (712) 255-3808

IDAHO

Boise Vet Center
5440 Franklin Road, Suite 1< Boise ID 83705

Pocatello Vet Center
1800 Garrett Way Pocatello ID 83201 (208)232-0316

ILLINOIS

Chicago Vet Center
7731 S. Halsted Street Chicago IL 60620
(773)962-3740

Chicago Heights Vet Center 1600 Halsted Street Chicago Heights IL 60411 (708) 754-0340

East St. Louis Vet Center 1265 N. 89th Street Suite 5 East St. Louis IL 62203 (618)397-6602

Evanston Vet Center 565 Howard St. Evanston IL 60202 (847)332-1019

Quad Cities Vet Center .
1529 46th Avenue #6 MolineIL 61265 (309)762-6954

Oak Park Vet Center 155 S. Oak Park Avenue Oak Park IL 60302 (708)383-3225

Peoria Vet Center 3310 N. Prospect Road Peoria IL 61603 (309) 688-2170

Springfield Vet Center
1227 S. Ninth Street Springfield IL 62703 (217) 492-4955

INDIANA

Evansville Vet Center
311 N. Weinbach Avenue Evansville IN 47711 (812)473-5993

Fort Wayne Vet Center 528 W. Berry Street Fort Wayne IN 46802 (260)460-1456

Indianapolis Vet Center 3833 N. Meridian Street Suite 120 Indianapolis IN 46208 (317)988-1600

Gary Area Vet Center
6505 Broadway Ave. Merrillville IN 46410 (219) 736-5633

KANSAS

Manhattan Vet Center 205 South 4th Street, Suite B Manhattan KS 66502 (785) 587-8257

Wichita Vet Center
251 N. Water St. Wichita KS 67202 (316)685-2221

Silver Spring Vet Center
1015 Spring Street, Suite 101 Silver Spring MD 20910 1-866-360-9094

MAINE

Bangor Vet Center
368 Harlow St. In-Town Plaza Bangor ME 04401 (207) 947-3391

Caribou Vet Center 456 York Street York Street Complex Caribou ME 04736 (207) 496-3900

Lewiston Vet Center
Parkway Complex 29 Westminster St. Lewiston ME 04240 (207) 783-0068

Portland Vet Center
475 Stevens Ave. Portland ME 04103 (207) 780-3584

Sanford Vet Center 628 Main Street Springvale ME 04083 (207) 490-1513

MICHIGAN

Dearborn Vet Center 2881 Monroe Street, Suite 100 Dearborn MI 48124 (313) 277-1428

Detroit Vet Center
4161 Cass Avenue Detroit MI 48201 (313)831-6509

Escanaba Vet Center
3500 Ludington Street Suite #110 Escanaba MI 49829 (906)

233-0244

Grand Rapids Vet Center 2050 Breton Rd SE Grand Rapids MI 49546 (616)285-5795

Saginaw Vet Center 4048 Bay Road Saginaw MI 48603 (989) 321-4650

MINNESOTA

Duluth Vet Center
405 E. Superior Street Duluth MN 55802 (218) 722-8654

St. Paul Vet Center 550 County Road D Suite 10 New Brighton MN 55112 (651) 644-4022

MISSOURI

Kansas City Vet Center 301 East Armour Blvd. Suite 305 Kansas City MO 64111 (816) 753-1866

St. Louis Vet Center 2901 Olive St. Louis MO 63103 (314)531-5355

MISSISSIPPI

Biloxi Vet Center
288 Veterans Ave Biloxi MS 39531 (228) 388-9938

Jackson Vet Center
1755 Lelia Dr., Suite 104 Jackson MS 39216 (601) 965-5727

MONTANA

Billings Vet Center 1234 Ave. C Billings MT 59102 (406) 657-6071

Missoula Vet Center
500 N. Higgins Avenue Suite 202
Missoula MT 59802 (406) 721-4918

NORTH CAROLINA

Charlotte Vet Center
2114 Ben Craig Dr., Suite 300 Charlotte NC 28262 (704) 549-8025

Fayetteville Vet Center
4140 Ramsey St., Suite 110 Fayetteville NC 28311 (910) 488-6252

Greensboro Vet Center
2009 S. Elm-Eugene St. Greensboro NC 27406 (336)333-5366

Greenville Vet Center
1021 WH Smith Blvd., Suite 10' Greenville NC 27834 (252) 355-7920

Raleigh Vet Center 1649 Old Louisburg Rd. Raleigh NC 27604 (919) 856-4616

NORTH DAKOTA

Fargo Vet Center
3310 Fiechtner Drive, Suite 100
Fargo ND 58103
(701) 237-0942

Minot Vet Center 1400 20th Avenue SW Minot ND 58701 (701)852-0177

NEBRASKA

Lincoln Vet Center 3119 O Street, Suite A Lincoln NE 68510 (402) 476-9736

Omaha Vet Center
2428 Cuming Street Omaha NE 68131 (402) 346-6735

NEW HAMPSHIRE

Berlin Vet Center

515 Main Street GorhamNH 03581 (603) 752-2571

Manchester Vet Center 103 Liberty St. Manchester NH 03104 (603) 668-7060

<u>NEW JERSEY</u>

Newark Vet Center 2 Broad St., Suite 703 Bloomfield NJ 07003 (973) 748-0980

Trenton Vet Center
934 Parkway Ave., Suite 201 Ewing NJ 08618 (609) 882-5744

Jersey City Vet Center
110A Meadowlands Pkwy Suite 102
Secaucus NJ 07094 (201)223-7787

Ventnor Vet Center
6601 Ventnor Ave., Suite 105, Ventnor Bldg. Ventnor NJ 08406 (609) 487-8387

<u>NEW MEXICO</u>

Albuquerque Vet Center
1600 Mountain Road NW Albuquerque NM 87104 (505) 346-6562

Farmington Vet Center
4251 E. Main Suite B Farmington NM 87402 (505) 327-9684

Las Cruces Vet Center
230 S. Water Street Las Cruces NM 88001 (575) 523-9826

Sante Fe Vet Center
2209 Brothers Road, Suite 110 Santa Fe NM 87505 (505) 988-6562

<u>NEVADA</u>

Las Vegas Vet Center 1919 S. Jones Blvd., Suite A Las Vegas NV 89146 (702) 251-7873

Reno Vet Center
1155 W. 4th Street, Suite 101 Reno NV 89503 (775) 323-1294

<u>NEW YORK</u>

Albany Vet Center
17 Computer Drive West Albany NY 12205 (518) 626-5130

Babylon Vet Center
116 West Main St. Babylon NY 11702 (631) 661-3930

Binghamton Vet Center
53 Chenango Street Binghamton NY 13901 (866) 716-8213

Bronx Vet Center
2471 Morris Avenue, Suite 1A Bronx NY 10468 (718) 367-3500

Brooklyn Vet Center
25 Chapel St., Suite 604 Brooklyn NY 11201 (718) 624-2765

Buffalo Vet Center
564 Franklin Street, 2nd Floor Buffalo NY 14202
(716) 882-0505

Nassau County Vet Center 970 South Broadway Hicksville NY 11801 (631) 661-3930

Middletown Vet Center
726 East Main Street, Suite 203 Middletown NY 10940 (845) 342-9917

Manhattan Vet Center
32 Broadway, 2nd Floor Suite 200 New York NY 10004 (212) 742-9591

Harlem Vet Center
2279 3rd Ave., 2nd Floor New York NY 10035 (212)426-2200

Rochester Vet Center
1867 Mount Hope Ave. Rochester NY 14620 (585) 232-5040

Staten Island Vet Center
150 Richmond Terrace Staten Island NY 10301 (718) 816-4499

Syracuse Vet Center 716 East Washington St. Suite 101
Syracuse NY 13210 (315)478-7127

Watertown Vet Center 210 Court Street Watertown NY 13601 (866) 610-0358

White Plains Vet Center
300 Hamilton Ave., 1st floor White Plains NY 10601 (914) 682-6250

Queens Vet Center
75-10B91 Ave. Woodhaven NY 11421 (718) 296-2871

OHIO

Cincinnati Vet Center
801B W 8th St., Suite 126 Cincinnati OH 45203 (513) 763-3500

Cleveland Vet Center
2022 Lee Road Cleveland OH 44118 (216) 932-8471

Columbus Vet Center
30 Spruce Street Columbus OH 43215 (614) 257-5550

Dayton Vet Center
6th Floor, East Medical Plaza 627 Edwin C. Moses Blvd. Dayton OH 45408
(937) 461-9150

Parma Vet Center
5700 Pearl Road, Suite 102 Parma OH 44129 (440) 845-5023

Toledo Vet Center
1565 S. Byrne Road, Suite 104 Toledo OH 43614 (419)213-7533

OKLAHOMA

Oklahoma City Vet Center
1024 NW 47th St, S. B Oklahoma City OK 73118 (405)4565184

Tulsa Vet Center
1408 S. Harvard Ave. Tulsa OK 74112 (918)748-5105

OREGON

Eugene Vet Center
1255 Pearl Street, Suite 200 Eugene OR 97402 (541)465-6918

Grants Pass Vet Center
211 S.E. 10th St. Grants Pass OR 97526 (541) 479-6912

Portland Vet Center
8383 N.E. Sandy Blvd. Suite #110 Portland OR 97220
(503)273-5370

Salem Vet Center

617 ChemeketaSt. NE Suite 100 Salem OR 97301
(503)362-9911

PENNSYLVANIA

DuBois Vet Center
100 Meadow Lane, Suite 8
DuBois PA 15801
(814) 372-2095

Erie Vet Center Renaissance Centre 1001 State St., Suite 102 Erie PA 16501 (814) 453-7955

Harrisburg Vet Center 1500 N. Second Street, Suite 2 Harrisburg PA 17102 (717) 782-3954

McKeesport Vet Center 2001 Lincoln Way McKeesport PA 15131 (412) 678-7704

Philadelphia Vet Center
801 Arch Street, Suite 102 Philadelphia PA 19107 (215) 627-0238

Philadelphia (NE) Vet Center
101 E. Olney Avenue
Philadelphia PA 19120

Pittsburgh Vet Center
2500 Baldwick Rd Pittsburgh PA 15205 (412)920-1765

Scranton Vet Center
1002 Pittston Ave Scranton PA 18505 (570) 344-2676

Williamsport Vet Center
49 E. Fourth Street, Suite 104
Williamsport PA 17701
(570) 327-5281

<u>PUERTO RICO</u>

Arecibo Vet Center
50 Gonzalo Marin St.
Arecibo PR 00612

(787) 879-4510

Ponce Vet Center
35 Mayor St., Suite 1 Ponce PR 00730 (787) 841-3260

San Juan Vet Center Cond. Medical Center Plaza Suite LC 8,9 8c 11, Urb. La Riviera
Rio Piedras PR 00921 (787) 749-4409

RHODE ISLAND

Providence Vet Center
2038 Warwick Ave Warwick RI 02889 (401) 739-0167

SOUTH CAROLINA

Columbia Vet Center
1513 Pickens St. Columbia SC 29201 (803) 765-9944

Greenville Vet Center
14 Lavinia Ave. Greenville SC 29601 (864)271-2711

Charleston Vet Center 5603-A Rivers Ave. N. Charleston SC 29406 (843) 747-8387

SOUTH DAKOTA

Pine Ridge Vet Center P.O. Box 910,105 E. Hwy 18 Martin, SD 57747 (605)685-1300

Rapid City Vet Center 621 6th St, Suite 101 Rapid City SD 57701 (605) 348-0077

Sioux Falls Vet Center
601 S. Cliff Ave., Suite C Sioux Falls SD 57104 (605)330-4552

TENNESSEE

Chattanooga Vet Center
951 Eastgate Loop Road Bldg 5700 - Suite 300 Chattanooga TN 37411 (423) 855-6570

Johnson City Vet Center
1615A Market St. Johnson City TN 37604 (423) 928-8387

Knoxville Vet Center
2817 E. Magnolia Ave. Knoxville TN 37914 (865) 545-4680

Memphis Vet Center 1407 Union Ave., Suite 410 Memphis TN 38104 (901) 544-0173

Nashville Vet Center
1420 Donelson Pike, Suite A-5 Nashville TN 37217 (615)366-1220

TEXAS

Amarillo Vet Center 3414 Olsen Blvd., Suite E Amarillo TX 79109 (806) 354-9779

Austin Vet Center
1110 West William Cannon Dr. Suite 301 Austin TX 78745 (512)416-1314

Corpus Christi Vet Center
4646 Corona, Suite 250 Corpus Christi TX 78411 (361) 854-9961

Dallas Vet Center
10501 N. Central, Suite 213 Dallas TX 75231 (214)361-5896

El Paso Vet Center
1155 Westmoreland, Suite 121 El Paso TX 79925 (915) 772-0013

Ft. Worth Vet Center
1305 W Magnolia St., Suite B Ft. Worth TX 76104 (817)921-9095

Killeen Heights Vet Center
302 Millers Crossing, Suite #4 Harker Heights TX 76548 (254) 953-7100

Houston Vet Center
2990 Richmond Ave., Suite 325 Houston TX 77098 (713)523-0884

Houston Vet Center
701 N. Post Oak Road, Suite 102 Houston TX 77024 (713)682-2288

Laredo Vet Center
6020 McPherson Road, Suite 1A Laredo TX 78041 (956) 723-4680

Lubbock Vet Center

3208 34th St. Lubbock TX 79410 (806) 792-9782

McAllen Vet Center 801 Nolana Loop, Suite 140 McAllen TX 78504 (956)631-2147

Midland Vet Center
2817 W. Loop 250 N., Suite E Midland TX 79705 (432) 697-8222

San Antonio Vet Center
231 W. Cypress St., S. 100 S. Antonio TX 78212 (210) 472-4025

UTAH

Provo Vet Center
1807 No. 1120 West Provo UT 84604 (801)377-1117

Salt Lake Vet Center
1354 East 3300 South Salt Lake UT 84106 (801)584-1294

VIRGINIA

Alexandria Vet Center
6940 South Kings Highway #204 Alexandria VA 22310
(703) 360-8633

Norfolk Vet Center
1711 Church Street, Suites A&B Norfolk VA 23504 (757)623-7584

Richmond Vet Center
4902 Fitzhugh Ave. Richmond VA 23230 (804)353-8958

Roanoke Vet Center
350 Albemarle Ave., SW Roanoke VA 24016 (540) 342-9726

VIRGIN ISLANDS

St. Croix Vet Center
The Village Mall, RR 2 Box 10553 Kingshill St. Croix VI 00850
(340) 778-5553

St. Thomas Vet Center
Buccaneer Mall, Suite #8 St. Thomas VI 00802 (340) 774-6674

VERMONT

South Burlington Vet Center

359 Dorset St. South Burlington VT 05403 (802) 862-1806

White River Junction Vet Center
Gilman Office, Building #2 222 Holiday Inn Drive White River Junction VT 0500 (802)295-2908

WASHINGTON

Bellingham Vet Center
3800 Bryon Ave, Suite 124 Bellingham WA 98229 (360) 733-9226

Everett Vet Center
3311 Wetmore Avenue Everett WA 98201 (425) 252-9701
Seattle Vet Center 2030-9th Ave., Suite 210 Seattle WA 98121 (206) 553-2706

Spokane Vet Center
100 No. Mullan Rd., Suite 102 Spokane WA 99206 (509) 444-8387

Tacoma Vet Center
4916 Center St., Suite E Tacoma WA 98409 (253) 565-7038

Yakima Valley Vet Center
2119 W.Lincoln Ave Yakima WA 98902 (509) 457-2736

WISCONSIN

Madison Vet Center
706 Williamson Street Madison WI 53703 (608) 264-5342

Milwaukee Vet Center
5401 N. 76th St. Milwaukee WI 53218 (414)536-1301

WEST VIRGINIA

Beckley Vet Center 1000 Johnstown Road Beckley WV 25801 (304) 252-8220

Charleston Vet Center

521 Central Avenue Charleston WV 25302 (304)343-3825

Huntington Vet Center
3135 16th Street Road, Suite 11 Huntington WV 25701 (304)523-8387

Martinsburg Vet Center
900 Winchester Avenue MartinburgWV 25401 (304) 263-6776

Morgantown Vet Center
1083 Greenbag Road Morgantown WV 26508 (304) 291-4303

Princeton Vet Center
905 Mercer Street Princeton WV 24740 (304) 425-5653

Wheeling Vet Center 1206 Chapline Street Wheeling WV 26003 (304) 232-0587

WYOMING

Casper Vet Center
1030 North Poplar Suite B Casper WY 82601 (307) 261-5355

Cheyenne Vet Center
3219 E. Pershing Blvd Cheyenne WY 82001 (307) 778-7370

0 10 20 30 40 50
MILES
Pusan Perimeter
Pohang
Taegu
Miryang
Chingdong
Masan
Paedun
Sachon
Pusan
KOREA

IV

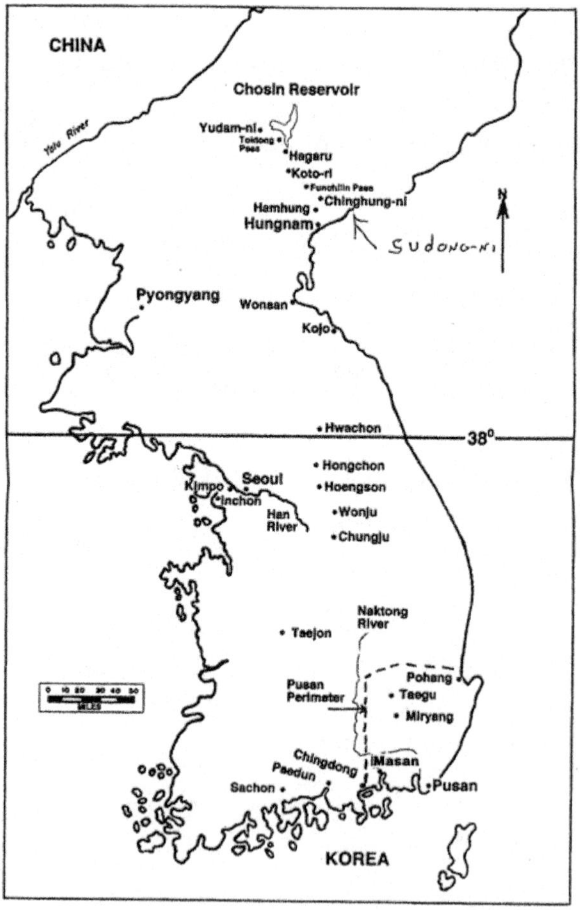
CHINA
Chosin Reservoir
Yalu River
Yudam-ni
Toktong Pass
Hagaru
Koto-ri
Funchilin Pass
Chinghung-ni
Hamhung
Hungnam
SUDONG-NI
N
Pyongyang
Wonsan
Kojo
Hwachon
38°
Hongchon
Hoengson
Seoul
Kimpo
Inchon
Han River
Wonju
Chungju
Naktong River
Taejon
0 10 20 30 40 50
MILES
Pusan Perimeter
Pohang
Taegu
Miryang
Chingdong
Masan
Paedun
Sachon
Pusan
KOREA

IV

Stan Modrak
Circa 1951 or 1952

Printed in Dunstable, United Kingdom

91228685R00050